School of the Prophets

Prophetic Training Manual

Wanda Roberson

Purpose Publishing LLC.
13194 US Highway 301 South, Suite 417
Riverview, Florida 33578

WWW.PURPOSEPUBLISHING.COM

DEDICATIONS

I dedicate this book to the first fruit of the School of the Prophets, my students in South Africa. You were the most amazing students. Your passion and drive to learn and grow in the prophetic was refreshing and inspiring. Thank you for allowing me to be a part of your journey.

To my husband, Dave Roberson, your unwavering love, prayers, and support have been a constant source of strength. I am deeply grateful for your belief in me and for always encouraging and challenging me to pursue my call.

To my mother, Barbara Sawyer—lovingly known as Mother Swayer. Throughout my life, you have been my strongest encourager, my confidant, a wonderful friend, and most importantly, my steadfast intercessor.

Special Thanks

To the Purpose Publishing family, I am deeply grateful for your professionalism and patience. Your dedication made this achievement a reality.

To my children, Raquel Barnes and Morgan Hanks. Your unwavering support and encouragement have meant the world to me throughout this journey.

To my awesome grandchildren, Madison, Kennedy, Natalie, and Jackson, my love for you knows no bounds.

To my sister, Aretha Swift, your encouragement, support, and inspiration have uplifted me in countless ways.

FOREWORD

Seasoned by God's grace, the author, Wanda Roberson, is a global and sought-after voice in the prophetic. Her ministry is far reaching and includes the development of prophetic training schools both nationally and internationally. She has graduated hundreds of students in the United States, different countries in Africa, and Canada. Her experience and expertise in prophetic training and activation are sure to be the catalysts that will catapult you to a higher level of understanding and execution in this area.

The prophetic has occupied a primary and enduring role within the biblical narrative, functioning not merely as a means of foretelling, but as a divinely appointed instrument for revelation, correction, encouragement, and alignment. From the Old Testament prophets to the New Testament Church, prophetic ministry has consistently served to communicate God's purposes and call His people into faithful response. As such, the prophetic warrants serious scriptural reflection, disciplined training, and responsible practice.

School of the Prophets Training Manual contributes meaningfully to this task. At a time when interest in prophetic ministry is widespread—often accompanied by both enthusiasm and misunderstanding—there is a clear need for resources that approach the prophetic with simplicity, rigor, biblical fidelity, and practical wisdom. Wanda Roberson addresses this need by offering a structured exploration of prophetic theology alongside practical instruction for discernment, development, and application. Rather than treating the prophetic predominantly as a heightened experiential phenomenon, Wanda brings clarity as she guides the reader to understand how prophetic ministry functions in relation to Scripture, the Holy Spirit, and the church. Particular attention is given to the development of the prophetic individual, emphasizing character, accountability, and scriptural coherence as essential components to operating within this divine space.

One of the notable strengths of School of The Prophets Training Manual is its balanced approach. The author neither dismisses the experiential dimension of the prophetic nor allows it to operate without discernment and evaluation. Instead, she presents the prophetic not only as a call but also as a discipline—one that can be cultivated through prayer, study, meditation and reflective practice. This perspective is especially valuable for those in training, as well as for readers seeking a clearer framework for understanding how the prophetic ministry functions.

School of the Prophetic Training Manual is a helpful best-practice resource for students, ministry practitioners, and educators who desire a thoughtful and responsible approach to prophetic training. It invites readers to move beyond curiosity, limitation or imitation toward a deeper comprehension of the prophetic that is shaped by Scripture, guided by Holy Spirit, with intentional accountability to God and the Body of Christ.

The School of The Prophets Training Manual offers a meaningful contribution to prophetic studies and provides a foundation for thoughtful engagement, practice and continued growth. I strongly recommend this literary expose' to those called to the five-fold ministry, prophets in training and to others who are simply seeking clarity in this area.

May God's blessing rest upon this tremendous work. I commend the author, Wanda Roberson, for this innovative production and the endless hours it took to produce ***School of The Prophets Training Manual.***

Dr. Josie Carr
CEO/Senior Consultant – DESTINY Educational Consultant
Author: The Power of Confidence: A framework for Your Success
Running After God, The Ultimate Pursuit

CONTENTS

CHAPTER 01
PROPHETIC INTERCESSION

2 Chronicles 7:14 (KJV):

"If my people, who are called by my name, shall humble themselves, and pray, and seek my face, and turn from their wicked ways; then will I hear from heaven, and will forgive their sin, and will heal their land."

1 Timothy 2:1–3 (KJV):
"I exhort therefore, first of all, supplications, prayers, intercessions, thanksgivings, be made for all men; for kings, and for all that are in authority; that we may lead a quiet and peaceable life in all godliness and honesty. For this is good and acceptable in the sight of God our Savior."

PRAYER

The Greek verb proseuchomai Strong's (#4336) and its noun form proseuchē (#4335) denote prayer in the general sense. This foundational word encompasses worship unto God—a posture of reverence, communion, and spiritual alignment.

WHAT IS PRAYER?

Prayer is communing with God.

Prayer is being relational with God.

Prayer is of the Spirit.

Prayer is waiting upon God.

Prayer is passion.

Prayer is a privilege.

Prayer is fellowship.

Prayer is intimacy.

Prayer is a command.

Prayer is power.

Prayer is a lifestyle.

Prayer is a discipline.

Purpose of Prayer!

PRAYER RELEASES GOD'S PLANS INTO THE EARTHLY REALM.

Prayer gives you access to Heaven.

Prayer allows us to minister to our God.

Prayer puts God to work on our behalf.

Prayer authorizes God to respond to our needs.

Prayer changes things on our behalf.

Prayer releases God to bring his will to life and establish his kingdom on earth.

Prayer allows us to hear God's voice.

Prayer brings us into obedience with the Word of God.

Prayer is the responsibility of every born-again believer.

Prayer gives us the authority to change circumstances and situations, causing the will of God to be fulfilled.

Prayer allows us to receive the desires of our hearts.

Prayer allows us to be delivered from those things that would hinder our walk with God.

Prayer helps us obtain supernatural power to overcome and overthrow the enemy.

Prayer acknowledges God. Then He can direct our paths and order our steps.

Prayer builds a hedge of protection around us.

Prayer gives us power and dominion over the works of the enemy.

Prayer allows us to embrace his purpose in our lives.

Prayer allows us to unlock the blessings of God.

Joshua 1:8 reminds us that spiritual success comes through meditating on God's Word—prayer and waiting deepen that connection.

PRAYING ALL TYPES OF PRAYERS

Ephesians 6:18 (KJV):
"Praying always with all prayer and supplication in the Spirit and watching thereunto with all perseverance and supplication for all saints."

We are admonished to pray specific types of prayers for particular situations.

Each type of prayer has a distinct function.

THE PRAYER OF AGREEMENT / CORPORATE

To symphonize or harmonize: It means a perfect agreement of the hearts, desires, wishes, and voices of two or more persons praying to God.

This type of prayer involves entering into agreement with two or more believers, along with the Word of God, to receive His manifested promises. One must be in harmony or agreement for this prayer to be effective.

Matthew 18:19 (KJV): "Again I say unto you that if two of you shall agree on earth as touching anything that they shall ask, it shall be done for them by my Father, who is in heaven."

Acts 1:14 (NKJV): "These all continued with one accord in prayer and supplication, with the women and Mary the mother of Jesus, and with His brothers."

Acts 2:42 (KJV) And they continued stedfastly in the apostles' doctrine and fellowship, and in breaking of bread, and in prayers."

Acts 12:5–13 (KJV): Peter: "Therefore was kept in prison; but prayer was made without ceasing by the church unto God for him."

The Prayer of Petition and Supplication

The Greek verb deomai (#1189) means "to have a need" and "ask God to meet a specific need." The noun deēsis (#1162) also means "to ask" but connotes urgency and necessity. It means a request, a petition which involves begging, an intense asking of God. "To make known one's need, urgently request, supplicate, beseech" (Bullinger, Lexicon).

This request can be made unto God in the form of a verbal and/or written petition.

Philippians 4:6 (NKJV): "Be anxious for nothing, but in everything, by prayer and supplication with thanksgiving, let your request be made known unto God."

Hebrews 5:7 (NKJV): "who, in the days of His flesh, when He had offered up prayers and supplications, with vehement cries and tears to Him who was able to save Him from death, and was heard because of His godly fear."

James 5:16 (KJV): "Confess your faults one to another, And pray one for another, that ye may be healed. The effectual fervent prayer of a righteous man availeth much."

1 Peter 3:12 (NKJV): "For the eyes of the Lord are on the righteous, and his ears open to their prayers: But the face of the Lord is against those who do evil."

The Prayer of Thanksgiving

The Greek word eucharistia denotes a prayer marked with deep thankfulness.

This form of prayer expresses gratitude and thanksgiving to God for all those things he has done.

Ephesians 5:20 (KJV): "Giving thanks always for all things unto God and the Father in the name of our Lord Jesus Christ."

Colossians 4:2 (NKJV): "Continue earnestly in prayer, being vigilant in it with thanksgiving."

Philippians 4:6 (NKJV): "Be anxious for nothing, but in everything by prayer and supplication, with thanksgiving, let your requests be made known to God."

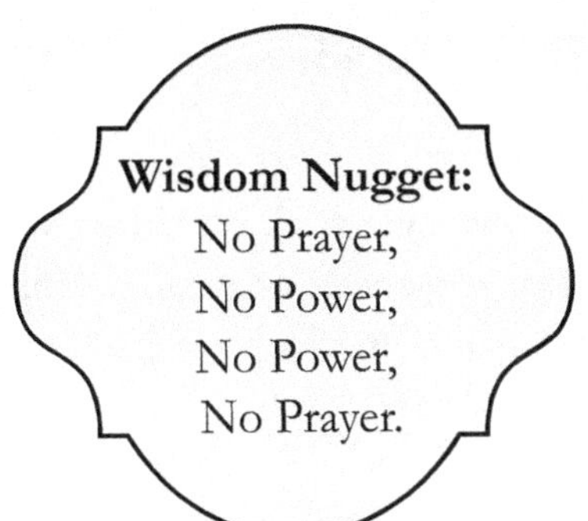

1 Timothy 2:1 (KJV):
"I exhort therefore, first of all, that supplications, prayers, intercessions, thanksgivings, be made for all men."

THE PRAYER OF BINDING AND LOOSING

This type of prayer empowers believers to declare what's bound or loosed, based on what God has declared bound or loosed in heaven and on earth.

Luke 9:1(NKJV): "Then He called His twelve disciples together and gave them power and authority over all demons, and to cure diseases."

Luke 10:19 (NKJV): "Behold, I give you the authority to trample on serpents and scorpions, and over all the power of the enemy, and nothing shall by any means hurt you."

The same authority that Jesus operated in has been given to every believer!

This prayer is based on the authority of God's Word.

You can bind evil spirits.

You can loose angelic spirits.

Matthew 18:18 (KJV): "Verily I say unto you, whatsoever ye shall bind on earth shall be bound in heaven, and whatsoever ye shall loose on earth shall be loosed in heaven."

Matthew 12:29 (KJV): "Or how can one enter into the house of the strong man, and spoil his goods, except he first bind the strong man? And then he will spoil his house."

THE PRAYER OF FAITH

This type of prayer involves boldly declaring or speaking a command, anchored in faith against a problem.

Faith released gives substance to what you don't see.

Hebrews 11:1 (KJV): "Now faith is the substance of things hoped for, the evidence of things not seen."

Mark 11:23–24 (KJV): "For verily I say unto you, That whosoever shall say unto this mountain, Be thou removed, and be thou cast into the sea; and shall not doubt in his heart, but shall believe that those things which he saith shall come to pass; he shall have whatsoever he saith."

Mark 11:24 (KJV): "Therefore I say unto you, what things soever ye desire, when ye pray, believe that ye receive them, and ye shall have them."

Faith is the driving force that activates this prayer and brings it to manifestation!

Hebrews 11:6 (NIV): "And without faith it is impossible to please God, because anyone who comes to him must believe that he exists and that he rewards those who earnestly seek him."

James 5:14 (NKJV): "Is any sick among you? Let him call for the elders of the church, and let them pray over him, anointing him with oil in the name of the Lord."

James 5:15 (NKJV): "And the prayer of faith shall save the sick, and the Lord shall raise him up; and if he has committed sins, they shall be forgiven him."

INTERCESSORY PRAYER

This kind of prayer is offered on behalf of others—individuals, families, communities, and even entire nations. In doing so, you posture yourself between God and the enemy, interceding on behalf of those in need.

01. **Timothy 2:1–4 (NKJV):** "Therefore I exhort first of all that supplications, prayers, intercessions, and giving of thanks be made for all men,"

02. "for kings and all who are in authority, that we may lead a quiet and peaceable life in all godliness and reverence."

03. "For this is good and acceptable in the sight of God our Savior,"

04. "who desires all men to be saved and to come to the knowledge of the truth."

INTERCESSION

Intercession—prayers offered to God on behalf of an individual, people group, city, state, or nation.

Purpose of Intercession: 1 Timothy 2:4 states that God wants everyone to be saved and to have an intimate relationship with Him. Intercession is a powerful form of prayer in which believers partner with God to stand in the gap on behalf of others, bringing salvation, healing, and restoration into their lives.

The heart of God is always to reconcile man unto himself … but he needs an intercessor that will stand in the gap.

God looks for an intercessor who is willing to stand in the gap to hold back the judgment for a city, nation, or people.

Isaiah 59:16 (NKJV): "He saw that there was no man, And wondered that there was no intercessor; Therefore His own arm brought salvation for Him; And His own righteousness, it sustained Him."

Wisdom Nugget: The heart of a prophet is birthed in Intercession!

Ezekiel 22:30 (KJV): "And I sought for a man among them, that he should make up the hedge, and stand in the gap before Me for the land, that I should not destroy it: but I found none."

To "intercede" means literally to "come in between."

Intercessor (Heb. pāgāʿ [paw-gah]): A mediator; a negotiator who acts as a link between both parties.

THE FRAMEWORK OF AN INTERCESSOR

Yielding to God regularly will increase your sensitivity to the Spirit.

An intercessor accepts the burden of the Lord: His concerns are your concerns. His heart is your heart.

Intercessors become co-labors of the Spirit as you stand in agreement with God.

An intercessor's life is characterized by selflessness and undying love.

Intercessors are summoned to stand as watchmen upon the wall, watching and praying.

An intercessor is clothed in humility. Although they are bold in the Spirit, they are meek, broken, and humble.

Intercessors value discretion above all, even when the Spirit reveals things to them.

Intercessors are not mouthy, full of gossip, backbiters, slanderous, or accusers of others.

Intercessors are mediators. They stand between heaven and earth on behalf of others.

Intercessors are not part of the fivefold ministry gift.

Intercession is not a grace gift—it's not one of the nine gifts given by the Holy Spirit.

We're all commanded to intercede, but not all will respond accordingly.

Intercessors will travail and give birth to what God is saying and doing.

Intercession always preceded a mighty move of God in the earth realm.

Your vision of his purpose will expand whenever you avail yourself to God through Intercession.

"Stands in the gap": he interposes himself in the breach made by the sin of God's people, thus holding back judgment.

"Makes up the hedge": by calling God's people back to repentance and obedience, he rebuilds their spiritual defenses.

Abraham Intercedes on Behalf of Cities

Gen 18:20–33

In Genesis 18:20–33, we see God purposed to destroy Sodom and Gomorrah because of their sins. However, Abraham's heart was to intercede on behalf of the people. His heart's cry as an intercessor was first for the restoration of a people, not destruction.

GENESIS 18:20–33 (NKJV)

20 And the Lord said, "Because the outcry against Sodom and Gomorrah is great, and because their sin is very grave,

21 I will go down now and see whether they have done altogether according to the outcry against it that has come to Me; and if not, I will know."

22 Then the men turned away from there and went toward Sodom, but Abraham still stood before the Lord.

23 And Abraham came near and said, "Would You also destroy the righteous with the wicked?

24 Suppose there were fifty righteous within the city; would You also destroy the place and not spare it for the fifty righteous that were in it?

25 Far be it from You to do such a thing as this, to slay the righteous with the wicked, so that the righteous should be as the wicked; far be it from You! Shall not the Judge of all the earth do right?"

26 So the Lord said, "If I find in Sodom fifty righteous within the city, then I will spare all the place for their sakes."

27 Then Abraham answered and said, "Indeed now, I who am but dust and ashes have taken it upon myself to speak to the Lord:

28 Suppose there were five less than the fifty righteous; would You destroy all of the city for lack of five?" So He said, "If I find there forty-five, I will not destroy it."

29 And he spoke to Him yet again and said, "Suppose there should be forty found there?" So He said, "I will not do it for the sake of forty."

30 Then he said, "Let not the Lord be angry, and I will speak: Suppose thirty should be found there?" So He said, "I will not do it if I find thirty there."

31 And he said, "Indeed now, I have taken it upon myself to speak to the Lord: Suppose twenty should be found there?" So He said, "I will not destroy it for the sake of twenty."

32 Then he said, "Let not the Lord be angry, and I will speak but once more: Suppose ten should be found there?" And He said, "I will not destroy it for the sake of ten."

33 So the Lord went His way as soon as He had finished speaking with Abraham; and Abraham returned to his place.

Aaron Stood as an Intercessor on Behalf of the Congregation of Israel

Numbers 16:46 (KJV): "And Moses said unto Aaron, Take thy censer, and put fire therein from off the altar, and lay incense thereon, and carry it quickly unto the congregation, and make atonement for them: for there is wrath gone out from Jehovah; the plague is begun."

Numbers 16:47 (KJV): "And Aaron took as Moses spake, and ran into the midst of the assembly; and, behold, the plague was begun among the people: and he put on the incense, and made atonement for the people."

Numbers 16:48 (KJV): "And he stood between the dead and the living, and the plague was stayed."

Moses and Aaron made atonement on behalf of Israel.

Atonement: "Condition of being at one (with others)," from atone. Later meanings include "reconciliation" (especially of sinners with God) and "propitiation of an offended party."

—*Online Etymology Dictionary,* © *2010 Douglas Harper*

Moses Provides the Perfect Example of an Intercessor on Behalf of a Nation

Exodus 32:7–14; Exodus 32:31–32 NKJV

He reminds God of His covenant with Abraham, Isaac, and Israel and pleads for mercy on behalf of the people.

7. "And the Lord said to Moses, 'Go, get down! For your people whom you brought out of the land of Egypt have corrupted themselves.

(8) They have turned aside quickly out of the way which I commanded them. They have made themselves a molded calf, and worshiped it and sacrificed to it, and said, 'This is your god, O Israel, that brought you out of the land of Egypt!' "

(9) "And the Lord said to Moses, 'I have seen this people, and indeed it is a stiff-necked people!

(10) Now therefore, let Me alone, that My wrath may burn hot against them and I may consume them. And I will make of you a great nation.'"

(11) Then Moses pleaded with the Lord his God, and said: "Lord, why does Your wrath burn hot against Your people whom You have brought out of the land of Egypt with great power and with a mighty hand?

(12) Why should the Egyptians speak, and say, 'He brought them out to harm them, to kill them in the mountains, and to consume them from the face of the earth'? Turn from Your fierce wrath, and relent from this harm to Your people.

(13) Remember Abraham, Isaac, and Israel, Your servants, to whom You swore by Your own self, and said to them, 'I will multiply your descendants as the stars of heaven; and all this land that I have spoken of I give to your descendants, and they shall inherit it forever.' "

(14) So the Lord relented from the harm which He said He would do to His people."

Moses Intercedes Once Again
on Behalf of Israel

Exodus 32:30–32 (NKJV): "Now it came to pass on the next day that Moses said to the people, 'You have committed a great sin. So now I will go up to the Lord; perhaps I can make atonement for your sin."

(31) Then Moses returned to the Lord and said, "Oh, these people have committed a great sin, and have made for themselves a god of gold!

(32) Yet now, if You will forgive their sin—but if not, I pray, blot me out of Your book which You have written."

The heart of an intercessor is revealed. Moses was willing to suffer the consequences for the sins of the people.

Jesus Is Our Chief Intercessor

Romans 8:34 (NKJV): "Who is he who condemns? It is Christ who died, and furthermore is also risen, who is even at the right hand of God, who also makes intercession for us."

Hebrews 7:25 (NKJV): "Therefore He is also able to save to the uttermost those who come to God through Him, since He always lives to make intercession for them."

Jesus Intercedes for His Disciples and Those to Come

John 17:1–26

John 17:20 (NKJV): "I do not pray for these alone, but also for those who will believe in Me through their word."

THE HOLY SPIRIT INTERCEDES ON OUR BEHALF

Romans 8:26–27 (NKJV): "Likewise the Spirit also helps in our weaknesses. For we do not know what we should pray for as we ought, *but the Spirit Himself makes intercession for us* with groanings which cannot be uttered. Now He who searches the hearts knows what the mind of the Spirit is because *He makes intercession for the saints according to the will of God.*"

DIFFERENT TYPES OF INTERCESSORS

People are called to intercede in many unique and specific ways, and there are various kinds of Intercessors, each standing in the gap for different needs and situations.

1. Issues Intercessors:

They stand against injustices and intercede over issues, such as abortion, homelessness, prostitution, etc. Their prayer-power mix often combines mercy and/or warfare to fight for those who can't fight for themselves.

2. List Intercessors:

This type of prayer warrior is someone who will pray about any subject you provide, but they're most comfortable following a written list. These intercessors are typically organized, methodical, and intentional—everything is documented.

» A List Intercessor: Ezra

3. Soul Intercessors:

These Intercessors are the spiritual midwives who help birth believers into the kingdom; when you get a revelation of hell and it terrifies you that you don't want to see anyone spend eternity there.

> » A Soul Intercessor: Paul (Acts 16:25–34)

4. Personal Intercessors:

These Intercessors have a deep passion for praying for leaders—pastors, business executives, and others in positions of influence. Their focus is personal, intentional, and often long-term. They frequently operate with a prayer mix that includes other anointings.

> » A Personal Intercessor: Mordecai (Book of Esther)

Colossians 1:9 (KJV): "For this cause we also, since the day we heard it, do not cease to pray for you, and to desire that ye might be filled with the knowledge of his will in all wisdom and spiritual understanding."

5. Financial Intercessors:

These Intercessors are summoned by God to call forth provision on behalf of others. You don't necessarily have to have an abundance of money to pray for others to be financially prosperous. Financial Intercessors will discern blockages that hinder prosperity and pray to move them.

> » A Financial Intercessor: Joseph—Gen 37–41

6. Mercy Intercessors:

They extend the mercy of God in prayer and deeds (Luke 10:30–37).

7. Crisis Intercessors:

They rush in and out of the throne room on behalf of others in crisis, acting as watchmen for God's people.

8. Warfare Intercessors:

They are the military might of prayer who fight to usher in truth by establishing God's authority in places where Satan has a stronghold on people (Matthew 11:12; 2 Corinthians10:4–6).

9. Worship Intercessors:

They release humanity's comforts and heaven's power as they usher in the presence of God through worship.

10. Government Intercessors:

They are watchmen who prayerfully uphold leaders in the church and in the political arena.

11. People Group and Israel Intercessors:

They pray for certain people/ethnic groups (Psalm 122:6).

12. Prophetic Intercessors:

They pray the things that are on God's heart and under his direction at that time for people, people groups, cities, nations, and a broad range of things. They pray, act upon the words, thoughts, images, and actions He releases at that given time.

Prophetic Intercession

Romans 8:26–27 (KJV): "Likewise, the Spirit also helpeth our infirmities; for we know not what we should pray for as we ought: but the Spirit itself maketh intercession for us with groanings, which cannot be uttered. And he that searcheth the hearts knoweth what is the mind of the Spirit because he maketh intercession for the saints according to the will of God."

The prophetic realm is that which speaks forth the mind, will, and counsel of God. It is the declaration of that which cannot be known by natural means.

In Romans 8:26, the word translated "intercession" is the Greek verb *huperentunchano*, which means "to intercede on behalf of another" or "to make a petition." In verse 27, the word is *entunchano,* meaning "to fall in with, meet with in order to converse," and by extension, "to make intercession."

When the prophetic and intercession are combined, you're praying the heart, mind, and will of God on earth.

WHAT IS PROPHETIC INTERCESSION?

Prophetic intercession is praying what is on the heart of God for a particular person, people group, city, or nation.

- Prophetic intercession is praying for the mind, will, and counsel of the Lord that reveals his plans and purpose through prayer in the Spirit.

- Prophetic intercession is not an office but is a body ministry.

- Prophetic intercession paves the way for the fulfillment of the prophetic promise.

- Prophetic intercession is an unction to pray, given by the Holy Spirit, for situations or circumstances about which you have very little knowledge in the natural.

- Prophetic Intercessors pray for the prayer requests that are on God's heart.

- Prophetic intercession is the ability to receive an immediate prayer request from God and pray about it in a divinely anointed utterance.

- Prophetic intercession is waiting before God to "hear" or receive God's burden—such as God's Word, His concern, warning, conditions, vision, or promises—responding to the Lord, and then to the people with appropriate actions.

ANNA: PICTURE OF A PROPHETIC INTERCESSOR

Anna is portrayed as a devoted intercessor in Luke 2:36–37 (NIV). Her passion and unwavering commitment to prayer are evident in how she never left the temple, serving night and day with fasting and prayers. Anna's life demonstrates a deep dedication to seeking God's will and being available to intercede for her people, embodying the heart of prophetic intercession.

36) "There was also a prophet, Anna, the daughter of Penuel, of the tribe of Asher. She was very old; she had lived with her husband seven years after her marriage,

(37) and then was a widow until she was eighty-four. She never left the temple but worshiped night and day, fasting and praying."

Prophetic intercession may be prompted when God is giving you an inner witness to pray. It is often coupled with a word of knowledge or a word of wisdom, bringing clarity and direction.

Spiritual gifts and manifestations of the Spirit are often at work to discern and detect things when needed.

Your intercession may become prophetic in nature and character when you are praying in the Spirit, and it carries the same anointing as one who prophesies the word of the Lord.

Prophetic people understand the times and seasons for prayer and release the will of God into the earth realm. 1 Chronicles 12:32 (NKJV): "Of the sons of Issachar who had understanding of the times, to know what Israel ought to do, their chiefs were two hundred; and all their brethren were at their command."

Prophetic people are in tune with God's eternal purposes and become sensitive to the Lord's voice and His operations.

CHAPTER 1 EXERCISE

ACTIVATION EXERCISE: ALLOW STUDENTS APPROXIMATELY 15 MINUTES TO COMPLETE ASSIGNMENTS.

Divide students into groups of four or five. Assign each group a specific type of prayer along with a matching scenario. For example: Prayer of Faith—Believing God for a Job. Remember, several prayers may be combined in this assignment. Have each group write a prayer for their assigned type of prayer, including relevant scripture references.

Upon completion, each group selects a spokesperson to read the prayer aloud.

Have students critique the prayer.

Critique should focus on whether the prayer is scripturally sound and aligned with the given scenario.

ACTIVATION EXERCISE:
ALLOW 15 MINUTES FOR EXERCISE.

Purpose: *to assist students in identifying their intercessory prayer mix. You are not confined to just one type of intercessor; rather, you may notice that you naturally flow between different kinds of prayer depending on the situation and the prompting of the Holy Spirit. By understanding the various types—such as mercy, crisis, warfare, worship, government, people group, and prophetic intercessors— you can better discern how God uses you in prayer and grow in confidence as you participate in each style.*

Group students by the type of intercessor they believe they are. If the group is larger than four people, split it. Assign the group to pray for a particular scenario based on how they have identified themselves. For example, Government Intercessors: Have them pray for a political figure in their city or country's government.

Ask them to pray in the Spirit for 2 or 3 minutes, then pray with understanding. Remember, everyone in that group must pray in unity concerning the scenario. Always ask the student what they sensed, heard, or saw during their prayer time. Allow each group to share.

Instructor: *Remember, not everyone in the class is a prophet; however, everyone can pray. Assist them in identifying the type of prayer mix they have.*

ACTIVATION EXERCISE:

Purpose: *to help you grow in praying prophetically and hearing the voice of God during prayer*

Prophetic Prayer
Form students into groups of two. Ask both people to pray in the Spirit for approximately two or three minutes. Ask them to become silent and listen to what God is saying. Then, without the other person saying anything, ask one person to pray what they sense God is showing them to pray over the other person. Now switch and allow the other person to pray what they sense God is showing them.

Instructor: *Encourage open sharing after each exercise. Ask the student: Was the prayer prayed over them accurate? Did it minister to them at the point of their need?*

Homework Exercise: *to be journaled and completed for the next class*

Group students together in groups of three. Assign the group a specific topic to intercede for, such as spiritual leaders, unbelievers, children, etc. They must contact their group and pray together (no more than ten to fifteen minutes) for their assignment. Journal what they heard, saw, or sensed during their time of prayer. Ask them to bring their journals to the next class and share their experience.

Prophetic Intercession
Chapter 1 Worksheet

Purpose: to understand the various types of prayers that are prayed for specific circumstances

1. What does it mean to pray all types of prayers?

____

____

____

____

____

2. Is there a particular type of prayer that you pray frequently? If so, what and why?

____

____

____

____

____

____

3. Which prayer is prayed on behalf of someone who is sick, and why?

____

____

____

____

____

4. Can two or more different types of prayers be prayed together? Explain.

____

____

____

____

____

5. If you personally desire something from God, which prayer would you pray? Why?

____

____

____

____

____

INTERCESSION

1. Can you remember a time when the Holy Spirit prompted you to intercede for a city, nation, or territory? Describe the experience.

____

____

____

____

2. What should your heart's motive be as an intercessor?

____

____

____

____

____

3. What two things kept God from destroying the children of Israel?

____

____

____

____

____

4. Is intercession an ascension gift given to the Body of Christ? Why or why not?

____

____

____

____

____

5. What type of intercessor has a heart to pray for leadership? Why?

____

____

____

____

____

6. Can you identify the type of intercessor you are?

____

____

____

____

____

7.Which types of intercessors have a passion to see unbelievers born into the Kingdom?

____

____

____

____

____

Prophetic Intercession

1. Does prophetic intercession differ from other types of intercession? If so, why?

____

____

____

____

____

2. Is praying in the Spirit necessary to flow in prophetic intercession?

____

____

____

____

____

3. How do you know when you're praying prophetically?

____

____

____

____

____

CHAPTER 02

HEARING THE VOICE OF GOD

Purpose:

To comprehend the various methods by which God uses to communicate his purpose and plans to mankind, thus challenging students to move in the realm of the Spirit so that they may hear the voice of the Lord

Prophecy is the ability to hear what God is saying and articulate that to a particular person, group, or nation.

John 10:3–5 (NKJV):
"To him the doorkeeper opens, and the sheep hear his voice; and he calls his own sheep by name and leads them out. And when he brings out his own sheep, he goes before them; and the sheep follow him, for they know his voice. Yet they will by no means follow a stranger, but will flee from him, for they do not know the voice of strangers."

John 10:27 (NKJV): "My sheep hear My voice, and I know them, and they follow Me."

Knowing the voice of God is essential for operating as a prophetic people!

THE NATURE OF PROPHETIC PEOPLE

1. Prophetic people are sensitive to the voice of God (John 10:27).

2. Prophetic people are trained to hear and understand the voice, counsel, and the mind of God (1 Corinthians 2:10–16; Isaiah 46:11; Psalm 29).

3. Prophetic people are intercessors and have a deep passion to see his kingdom revealed in the earth realm (Romans 8:25–26; Mathew 6:10).

4. Prophetic people flow out of the rest of God and are not moved by current world events and popular trends in today's world news (Hebrews 3:7; 4:11).

5. Prophetic people have the words that are relevant and stabilizing for our day and time (Isaiah 33:6).

6. Prophetic people understand and discern the times and seasons, just as the sons of Issachar (1 Chr 12:32).

7. Prophetic people understand that God reveals his secret to His prophets (Hebrews 12:28; Amos 3:7; Matthew 4:4).

8. Prophetic people are intimate with God (Revelation 4:11).

Discerning the Voice of God

There are many different voices on the earth realm, and prophetic people must learn to discern the voice of God.

1 Corinthians 2:14 (NIV): "The person without the Spirit does not accept the things that come from the Spirit of God but considers them foolishness and cannot understand them because they are discerned only through the Spirit."

Hebrews 5:14 (NKJV): "But solid food belongs to those who are of full age, that is, those who by reason of use have their senses exercised to discern both good and evil.

Discern:

To see or understand the difference; to make a distinction; as to discern between good and evil, truth, and falsehood. https://kingjamesbibledictionary.com

Discernment:

Discernment, in its simplest biblical sense, is the ability to make careful distinctions—between truth and error, good and evil, wisdom and folly. The Greek word often translated as "discern" in the New Testament is anakrino, meaning "to distinguish, to separate by diligent search, to examine." https://www.shepherdthoughts.com

Hebrews 4:12 instructs us that the Word of God discerns the thoughts and intentions of one's heart.

Four Voices That Speak to Us

1. Our Human spirit:

As humans, we are created as tripartite beings—spirit, soul, and body. We are spirit beings (1 Thess. 5:23)! God communicates with us directly through our spirit, from His spirit.

2. Holy Spirit:

Holy Spirit lives within every believer, acting as God's presence in our lives. This means the Holy Spirit not only resides in us but also actively communicates with and through us.

1 Corinthians 3:16: "Do you not know that you are God's temple and that God's Spirit dwells in you?"

Holy Spirit's Purposes:

- » To guide us
- » To comfort us
- » To teach us
- » To empower us to live out God's will

Holy Spirit helps us discern truth from error by making God's voice known in our hearts.

3. Evil spirits:

Evil spirits, also known as demonic or unclean spirits, attempt to communicate with us from the spiritual realm (the second Heaven). In Matthew 4:3–6, the devil (Satan) tries to tempt Jesus by twisting Scripture and appealing to His physical needs and desires.

Evil spirits' Purposes:

- » To deceive you
- » To tempt you
- » To lead God's people away from His truth and purpose

Evil spirits use various methods, such as the following:

- » Manipulation
- » Lies
- » Distorting Scripture
- » Fear

1 John 4:1 warns believers to "test the spirits" to determine whether they are from God, because many false prophets and deceiving spirits have gone out into the world.

4. Angels:

Angels are spiritual beings who serve as messengers and ministers for God. Angels speak to us on God's behalf, sharing messages and guidance on matters important to Him.

Hebrews 1:14 (NIV): "Are not all angels ministering spirits sent to serve those who will inherit salvation?"

Angels convey messages in various ways:

- » Through dreams and visions, providing insight or warnings from God

- » By personal encounters, where people experience direct interaction or receive guidance

- » Through scripture—helping to illuminate or clarify God's word

- » By ministering encouragement, provision, or protection, as seen in biblical accounts (e.g., encouraging Jesus in Gethsemane in Luke 22:43, providing for Elijah in 1 Kings 19:5–7, and protecting Daniel in Daniel 6:22)

Prophetic people are relentless in their pursuit to communicate with God!

HINDRANCES TO HEARING THE VOICE OF GOD

1 John 5:14–15 (NKJV): "Now this is the confidence that we have in Him, that if we ask anything according to His will, He hears us. And if we know that He hears us, whatever we ask, we know that we have the petitions that we have asked of Him."

Numerous obstacles can interfere with your capacity to discern God's voice. 1 Corinthians 16:13 (NIV) admonishes us to "Be on guard. Stand firm in the faith. Be courageous. Be strong."

1. **Fear:** 2 Tim1:7; 1 John 4:18; Psalm 54:6; Psalms 34:4

2. **Doubt and Unbelief:** Matthew 13:58

3. **Lack of Knowledge:** Proverbs1:5; Psalms 119:66; James1:5; 2 Timothy 2:15

4. **Lack of Intimacy with God:** Psalms 63:1–11; James 4:8; Colossians 3:1

5. **Lack of Confidence in Your Ability to Hear:** Philippians 4:13; Deuteronomy 31:6; Proverbs 3:26; Proverbs 3:5–6; Proverbs 14:26

6. **Comparing Yourself to Others:** 2 Corinthians 10:12; Romans 12:2; Psalm 139:14; John 1:3

7. **Lack of Faith:** Romans 1:17; 2 Corinthians 5:7; 1 John 5:4; Ephesians 2:8–9

8. **Pride:** Hebrews 3:15

> » Be still (Psalm 46:10)!

> » Practice the art of listening. Quiet your mind (Isaiah 50:4)!

> » Expect to hear the voice of God.

> » Focus your heart and mind on Jesus during your quiet time. Your heart must be properly focused.

> » Be confident in knowing that God desires to speak to you.

> » God's voice often comes as a flow of spontaneous thoughts.

> » Follow the Peace of God (Colossians 3:15)!

Ways in Which God Communicates

Throughout the Bible, God has always communicated with mankind, and He still desires fellowship with His creation. From Genesis, where God spoke directly to Adam and Eve, to the prophets, apostles, and countless individuals, SCRIPTURE reveals a consistent pattern of God reaching out to His people.

God Speaks Through His Word—Scripture

God can speak to you directly through His Word, whether you're reading the Bible or hearing it being preached. The Holy Spirit can bring you an understanding of the Word for direction, correction, and confirmation.

Intimacy is the birthplace of effective communication!

2 Timothy 3:16–17 (NKJV): "All scripture is given by inspiration of God and is profitable for doctrine, for reproof, for correction, for instruction in righteousness: that the man of God may be perfect, thoroughly furnished unto all good works."

Psalms 119:105 (NKJV): "Your word is a lamp to my feet And a light to my path."

God Speaks to Us Through Godly Counsel

Proverbs 11:14 (NKJV): "Where no counsel is, the people fall: but in the multitude of counsellors there is safety."

Proverbs 24:6 (KJV): "For by wise counsel thou shalt make thy war: and in multitude of counsellors there is safety."

Proverbs 12:15 (KJV): "The way of a fool is right in his own eyes: but he that hearkeneth unto counsel is wise."

Proverbs 20:18 (KJV): "Every purpose is established by counsel: and with good advice make war."

Proverbs 28:26 (KJV): "He that trusteth in his own heart is a fool: but whoso walketh wisely, he shall be delivered."

God Speaks in an Audible Voice

1 Samuel 3:4 (KJV): "That the LORD called Samuel: and he answered, Here am I."

1 Samuel 3:5 (KJV): "And he ran unto Eli, and said, Here am I; for thou calledst me. And he said, I called not; lie down again. And he went and lay down."

1 Samuel 3:6 (KJV): "And the LORD called yet again, Samuel. And Samuel arose and went to Eli, and said, Here am I; for thou didst call me. And he answered, I called not, my son; lie down again."

1 Samuel 3:7 (KJV): "Now Samuel did not yet know the LORD, neither was the word of the LORD yet revealed unto him."

1 Samuel 3:8 (KJV): "And the LORD called Samuel again the third time. And he arose and went to Eli, and said, Here am I; for thou didst call me. And Eli perceived that the LORD had called the child."

1 Samuel 3:9 (KJV): "Therefore Eli said unto Samuel, Go, lie down: and it shall be, if he call thee, that thou shalt say, Speak, LORD; for thy servant heareth. So Samuel went and lay down in his place."

1 Samuel 3:10 (KJV): "And the LORD came, and stood, and called as at other times, Samuel, Samuel. Then Samuel answered, Speak; for thy servant heareth."

1 Samuel 3:19 (KJV): "And Samuel grew, and the LORD was with him, and did let none of his words fall to the ground."

1 Samuel 3:20 (KJV): "And all Israel from Dan even to Beersheba knew that Samuel was established to be a prophet of the LORD."

1 Samuel 3:21 (KJV): "And the LORD appeared again in Shiloh: for the LORD revealed himself to Samuel in Shiloh by the word of the LORD."

He Spoke with Adam and Eve

Genesis 3:8 (NKJV): "And they heard the voice of the LORD God walking in the garden in the cool of the day: and Adam and his wife hid themselves from the presence of the LORD God amongst the trees of the garden."

Genesis 3:9: "And Jehovah God called unto the man, and said unto him, Where art thou?"

Genesis 3:9 (NKJV) Then the LORD God called to Adam and said to him, "Where are you?"

Genesis 3:10: "And he said, I heard thy voice in the garden, and I was afraid, because I was naked; and I hid myself."

Genesis 3:10 (NKJV): "So he said, 'I heard Your voice in the garden, and I was afraid because I was naked; and I hid myself.'"

He Spoke to Moses with an Audible Voice

Exodus 3:2 (NKJV): "And the Angel of the LORD appeared to him in a flame of fire from the midst of a bush. So he looked, and behold, the bush was burning with fire, but the bush was not consumed."

Exodus 3:3 (NKJV): "Then Moses said, 'I will now turn aside and see this great sight, why the bush does not burn.'"

Exodus 3:4 (NKJV): "So when the LORD saw that he turned aside to look, God called to him from the midst of the bush and said, 'Moses, Moses!' And he said, 'Here I am.'"

Exodus 3:5 (NJKV): "Then He said, 'Do not draw near this place. Take your sandals off your feet, for the place where you stand is holy ground.'"

Exodus 3:6 (NKJV): "Moreover He said, 'I am the God of your father—the God of Abraham, the God of Isaac, and the God of Jacob.' And Moses hid his face, for he was afraid to look upon God."

PAUL HEARD AN AUDIBLE VOICE

Acts 9:4 (NKJV): "Then he fell to the ground, and heard a voice saying to him, 'Saul, Saul, why are you persecuting Me?'"

Acts 9:5 (NKJV): "And he said, 'Who are You, Lord?' Then the Lord said, 'I am Jesus, whom you are persecuting. It is hard for you to kick against the goads.'"

JESUS HEARD AN AUDIBLE VOICE FROM HIS FATHER

Mark 1:11 (KJV): "And there came a voice from heaven, saying, Thou art my beloved Son, in whom I am well pleased."

Still Small Voice / Inner Witness

The "still small voice" is often referred to as the "inner voice" or the "inner witness." This is when God speaks through the inner declarations by His Spirit to yours.

Inner Witness: The inner witness is a term for the Holy Spirit's direct communication to your human spirit, often described as a spiritual impression frequently bypassing the physical senses. It is not heard in the normal way through the ears, but felt or sensed inwardly deep within your spirit.

The inner witness is almost like a feeling. It might be called a perception or that still small voice, but it is more like that sense of unexplainable knowing that something is right or wrong. You find yourself agreeing with it, but you don't always know why. **Romans 9:1 (NIV):** "I speak the truth in Christ—I am not lying, my conscience confirms it through the Holy Spirit."

HE SPOKE TO ELIJAH

1 Kings 19:11 (KJV): "And he said, Go forth, and stand upon the mount before the LORD. And, behold, the LORD passed by, and a great and strong wind rent the mountains, and brake in pieces the rocks before the LORD; but the LORD was not in the wind: and after the wind an earthquake; but the LORD was not in the earthquake:"

1 Kings 19:12 (KJV): "And after the earthquake a fire; but the LORD was not in the fire: and after the fire a still small voice."

1 Kings 19:13 (KJV): "And it was so, when Elijah heard it, that he wrapped his face in his mantle, and went out, and stood in the entering in of the cave. And, behold, there came a voice unto him, and said, What doest thou here, Elijah?"

Dreams

Acts 2:17 (KJV): "And it shall come to pass in the last days, saith God, I will pour out of my Spirit upon all flesh: and your sons and your daughters shall prophesy, and your young men shall see visions, and your old men shall dream dreams:"

Acts 2:17 (KJV): "And it shall come to pass in the last days, saith God, I will pour out of my Spirit upon all flesh: and your sons and your daughters shall prophesy, and your young men shall see visions, and your old men shall dream dreams:"

Dream: The Greek word *enupnion* (Strong's #1798) defines dreams as "something seen in sleep or a vision in a dream"—a succession of images or ideas present in the mind during sleep.

Dreams are formed in the mind of a man or woman from images and symbols that are unique to that individual, shaped by their background, experiences, and current life circumstances.

Dreams can originate in the natural mind or can be given as a message from God.

I encourage you to maintain a dream journal and record your dreams. As you grow in hearing God's voice, you will begin to recognize the various ways in which God speaks.

GOD SPOKE TO JOSEPH

Genesis 37:5 (NKJV): "Now Joseph had a dream, and he told it to his brothers; and they hated him even more."

Genesis 37:6 (NKJV): "So he said to them, 'Please hear this dream which I have dreamed:'"

Genesis 37:7 (NKJV): "There we were, binding sheaves in the field. Then behold, my sheaf arose and also stood upright; and indeed, your sheaves stood all around and bowed down to my sheaf."

Genesis 37:8 (NKJV): "And his brothers said to him, 'Shall you indeed reign over us? Or shall you indeed have dominion over us?' So they hated him even more for his dreams and for his words."

Genesis 37:9 (NKJV): "Then he dreamed still another dream and told it to his brothers, and said, 'Look, I have dreamed another dream. And this time, the sun, the moon, and the eleven stars bowed down to me.'"

GOD SPOKE TO ABIMELECH IN A DREAM

Genesis 20:3–5 (NKJV): "But God came to Abimelech in a dream by night, and said to him, 'Indeed you are a dead man because of the woman whom you have taken, for she is a man's wife.'"

Genesis 20:4 (NKJV): "But Abimelech had not come near her; and he said, 'Lord, will You slay a righteous nation also?'"

Genesis 20:5 (NKJV): "Did he not say to me, 'She is my sister'? And she, even she herself said, 'He is my brother.' In the integrity of my heart and innocence of my hands I have done this."

Visions

Visions: The act or power of perceiving abstract or invisible subjects as clearly as if they were visible objects. Vision means "to see" and is also defined as foresight. Visions from God are heavenly scenes supernaturally imposed on the eyes and mind while one is awake or asleep.

Hosea 12:10 (NKJV): "I have also spoken by the prophets, And have multiplied visions; I have given symbols through the witness of the prophets."

» **Hebrew:** *chāzôn* (Strong's #2377): a prophetic vision or divine revelation.

» **Greek:** *horáō* (Strong's #3708): properly "to see," often used metaphorically to mean seeing with the mind (i.e., spiritual perception); to perceive inwardly.

» **Greek:** *hórasis* (Strong's #3706): the act of gazing; an inspired appearance.

Elisha prayed for the Lord to open his servant's eyes to see into the realm of the Spirit. He received an open vision.

2 KINGS 6:14–17

2 Kings 6:14 (NKJV): "Therefore, he sent horses and chariots and a great army there, and they came by night and surrounded the city."

2 Kings 6:15 (NKJV): "And when the servant of the man of God arose early and went out, there was an army surrounding the city with horses and chariots. And his servant said to him, "Alas, my master! What shall we do?"

2 Kings 6:16 (NKJV): "So he answered, 'Do not fear, for those who are with us are more than those who are with them.'"

2 Kings 6:17 (NKJV): "And Elisha prayed, and said, 'Lord, I pray, open his eyes that he may see.' Then the Lord opened the eyes of the young man, and he saw. And behold, the mountain was full of horses and chariots of fire all around Elisha."

GOD SPOKE TO PAUL IN A VISION TO GIVE COMFORT

Acts 18:9–10 (NKJV): "Now the Lord spoke to Paul in the night by a vision, 'Do not be afraid, but speak, and do not keep silent; for I am with you, and no one will attack you to hurt you; for I have many people in this city.'"

An angel was sent to Cornelius in a vision with clear directions, instructing him to send men to Joppa to find Simon Peter. The angel specified that Peter was staying with Simon, a tanner, whose house was by the sea. This divine guidance set in motion the events that would bring Peter to Cornelius and ultimately lead to a significant expansion of the Gospel to the Gentiles.

Acts 10:1 (KJV): "There was a certain man in Caesarea called Cornelius, a centurion of the band called the Italian band,"

Acts 10:2 (KJV): "A devout man, and one that feared God with all his house, which gave much alms to the people, and prayed to God always."

Acts 10:3 (KJV): "He saw in a vision evidently about the ninth hour of the day an angel of God coming in to him, and saying unto him, Cornelius."

Acts 10:4 (KJV): "And when he looked on him, he was afraid, and said, What is it, Lord? And he said unto him, Thy prayers and thine alms are come up for a memorial before God."

Acts 10:5 (KJV): "And now send men to Joppa, and call for one Simon, whose surname is Peter."

Acts 10:6 (KJV): "He lodgeth with one Simon a tanner, whose house is by the sea side: he shall tell thee what thou oughtest to do."

Acts 10:7 (KJV): "And when the angel which spake unto Cornelius was departed, he called two of his household servants, and a devout soldier of them that waited on him continually."

Acts 10:8 (KJV): "And when he had declared all these things unto them, he sent them to Joppa."

Peter Received a Vision That Transformed His Perspective on the Gentile People

In Acts 10:9-35, Peter experienced a vision from God that dramatically shifted his perspective about the inclusion of Gentiles in the gospel message. As a result of the vision, Peter made a profound statement in verses 34-35: "I now realize how true it is that God does not show favoritism but accepts from every nation the one who fears him and does what is right." NIV

Acts 10:9 (KJV): "On the morrow, as they went on their journey, and drew nigh unto the city, Peter went up upon the housetop to pray about the sixth hour:"

Acts 10:10 (KJV): "And he became very hungry, and would have eaten: but while they made ready, he fell into a trance,"

Acts 10:11 (KJV): "And saw heaven opened, and a certain vessel descending unto him, as it had been a great sheet knit at the four corners, and let down to the earth:"

Visions are given for a purpose! They are one of the ways God reveals his purpose and will to mankind.

>> A vision brought Abram encouragement, hope, and comfort regarding an heir (Genesis 15:1–6).

>> God revealed to Samuel—through a vision—the pending judgment against Eli (1 Samuel 3:1–18).

>> Daniel received the interpretation of a dream through a night vision (Daniel 2:19).

>> Zacharias received a vision to announce the calling upon his Son John's life (Luke 1:22).

>> The women saw a vision of angels announcing Jesus was alive (Luke 24:23).

>> Ananias received instructions and guidance in a vision of where to locate Saul (Acts 9:10).

>> Paul received a vision to go to Macedonia and preach the Gospel (Acts 16:9).

CHAPTER 2 EXERCISE

ACTIVATION EXERCISE: ALLOW 20 MINUTES FOR THIS EXERCISE.

Purpose: *to develop students in their ability to discern God's voice*

Spiritual Activation: *Ask students to pray in the Spirit for two minutes, then quiet themselves for one minute. Listen to hear what the Spirit of God is speaking to you. Write down everything you hear, see, or the impression you received.*

Now practice this daily for three to five minutes, and don't forget to record everything you receive.

Purpose: *to develop students' ability to release the first impression of what they hear without allowing them time to think about it*

Spiritual Activation: *Select 6–8 students to line up in front of the class. Select one student at a time to release a word to each student. Don't allow them an opportunity to think. Take their hand and move them swiftly down the line. As they move down the line, they are to say ONLY one word to each person of what they're perceiving. You may not be able to utilize all the students. However, this exercise may carry over to the next class.*

Hearing the Voice of God
Chapter 2 Worksheet

Purpose: to comprehend the various methods by which God uses to communicate his purpose and plans to mankind, thus challenging students to move in the realm of the spirit so that they may hear the voice of the Lord.

John 10:27 (NKJV): "My sheep hear My voice, and I know them, and they follow Me."

1. What is prophecy?

____

____

____

____

____

____

2. Prophetic people are___________________**to the voice of**___________________

___________________**1.(John 10:27).**

3. Prophetic people are___________________**and have a**___________________

___________________**to see His**___________________**revealed in the**

earth realm (Romans 8:25–26; Matt. 6:10).

4. Complete the following statement. Prophetic people are:

       a) ___________________________________

       b) ___________________________________

       c) ___________________________________

       d) ___________________________________

5. Explain the difference between discernment and Discerning of spirits.

____

____

____

____

____

____

6. There are four voices that speak to us. List them below.

    a) ____

    b) ____

    c) ____

    d) ____

7. List four hindrances that prevent you from hearing God.

    a) ____

    b) ____

    c) ____

    d) ____

8. What obstacles have you encountered that have hindered you from hearing God?

____

____

____

____

____

9. Describe four methods by which God chooses to communicate with us.

    a) ____

       ____

    b) ____

       ____

c) ____

____

d) ____

____

10. What methods has God used to communicate with you? List and explain.

____

____

____

____

____

____

____

List three principles you received that were meaningful to you in this teaching.

a) ____

____

____

____

____

b) ____

____

____

____

c) ____

____

____

____

____

Notes:

CHAPTER 03
GIFTS OF THE HOLY SPIRIT

Purpose:
To gain insight, understanding, and revelation to identify and function in the grace gifting that's upon your life.

Every believer is to desire spiritual gifts.

1 Corinthians 12:31 (NKJV): "But earnestly desire the best gifts. And yet I show you a more excellent way."

1 Corinthians 14:1 (NKJV): "Pursue love, and desire spiritual gifts, but especially that you may prophesy."

NINE GIFTS OF THE SPIRIT IMPARTED BY THE HOLY SPIRIT:

1 Corinthians 12:1 (NKJV): "Now concerning spiritual gifts, brethren, I do not want you to be ignorant."

1 Corinthians 12:4 (NKJV): "There are diversities of gifts, but the same Spirit."

1 Corinthians 12:5 (NKJV): "There are diversities of gifts, but the same Spirit."

1 Corinthians 12:6 (NKJV): "There are differences of ministries, but the same Lord, but it is the same God who works all in all."

1 Corinthians 12:7 (NKJV): "But the manifestation of the Spirit is given to each one for the profit of all."

1 Corinthians 12:8 (NKJV): "For to one is given the word of wisdom through the Spirit, to another the word of knowledge through the same Spirit:"

1 Corinthians 12:9 (NKJV): "to another faith by the same Spirit, to another gifts of healings by the same Spirit,"

1 Corinthians 12:10 (NKJV): "to another the working of miracles, to another prophecy, to another discerning of spirits, to another different kinds of tongues, to another the interpretation of tongues."

1 Corinthians 12:11 (NKJV): "But one and the same Spirit works all these things, distributing to each one individually as He wills."

CHARACTERISTICS OF GIFTS

» The Holy Spirit gives gifts as he wills. You can't choose which gifts you desire (1 Cor. 12:11).

» Spiritual Gifts cannot be earned (Ephesians 4:7).

» Spiritual Gifts are freely given. They cannot be purchased or bargained for (Romans 12:6).

» Gifts are given to serve the Body of Christ (1 Pet. 4:10).

» All Gifts are supernatural.

» Gifts can and do operate in conjunction with other gifts.

» All Gifts were in operation in the Old Testament except Tongues and Interpretation of Tongues.

» Gifts operate by faith and are motivated by love.

Spiritual Gifts Are Divided into Three Distinct Categories

REVELATORY GIFTS: THEY REVEAL SOMETHING

Word of Wisdom: A supernatural revelation by the Spirit of God concerning the divine purposes and plans in the mind and will of God. (I Cor. 12:8)

Characteristics of the Word of Wisdom

It is a word/fragment from the full council of God.

It always speaks to or references the future.

OLD TESTAMENT EXAMPLES OF THE WORD OF WISDOM:

Noah was told about the flood 120 years before it happened.

Gen 6:13 (KJV): "And God said unto Noah, The end of all flesh is come before me; for the earth is filled with violence through them; and, behold, I will destroy them with the earth."

Gen 6:17 (KJV): "And, behold, I, even I, do bring a flood of waters upon the earth, to destroy all flesh, wherein is the breath of life, from under heaven; and everything that is in the earth shall die."

Gen 6:18 (KJV): "But with thee will I establish my covenant; and thou shalt come into the ark, thou, and thy sons, and thy wife, and thy sons' wives with thee."

Lot was warned of the destruction of Sodom and Gomorrah.

Genesis 19:13 (NKJV): "for we will destroy this place, because the cry of them is waxed great before Jehovah: and Jehovah hath sent us to destroy it." "For we will destroy this place, because the outcry against them has grown great before the face of the LORD, and the LORD has sent us to destroy it."

Genesis 19:14 (NKJV): "And Lot went out, and spake unto his sons-in-law, who married his daughters, and said, Up, get you out of this place; for Jehovah will destroy the city. But he seemed unto his sons-in-law as one that mocked. "So Lot went out and spoke to his sons-in-law, who had married his daughters, and said, "Get up, get out of this place; for the LORD will destroy this city!" But to his sons-in-law he seemed to be joking."

Genesis 19:15 (NKJV): "And when the morning arose, then the angels hastened Lot, saying, Arise, take thy wife, and thy two daughters that are here, lest thou be consumed in the iniquity of the city." Another translation reads: "When the morning dawned, the angels urged Lot to hurry, saying, 'Arise, take your wife and your two daughters who are here, lest you be consumed in the punishment of the city.'"

Joel prophesied that God's Spirit would be poured out upon all flesh in the last days. This was a word of wisdom.

Joel 2:27 (NKJV): "Then you shall know that I am in the midst of Israel: I am the LORD your God and there is no other. My people shall never be put to shame."

Joel 2:28 (NKJV): "And it shall come to pass afterward That I will pour out My Spirit on all flesh; Your sons and your daughters shall prophesy, Your old men shall dream dreams, Your young men shall see visions."

Joel 2:29 (NKJV): "and also upon the servants and upon the handmaids in those days will I pour out my Spirit." "And also on My menservants and on My maidservants I will pour out My Spirit in those days."

Oftentimes, the Word of Wisdom and the Word of Knowledge operate together with the Gift of prophecy.

New Testament Examples of the Word of Wisdom

Agabus prophesied and released a word of wisdom about a coming famine and drought.

Acts 11:28 (KJV): "And there stood up one of them named Agabus and signified by the Spirit that there should be a great famine over all the world: which came to pass in the days of Claudius."

Paul received a word of wisdom from an Angel of the Lord.

Acts 27:21 (NKJV) "But after long abstinence from food, then Paul stood in the midst of them and said, 'Men, you should have listened to me, and not have sailed from Crete and incurred this disaster and loss.'"

Acts 27:22 (NKJV): "And now I urge you to take heart, for there will be no loss of life among you, but only of the ship."

Acts 27:23 (NKJV): "For there stood by me this night an angel of the God to whom I belong and whom I serve,"

Acts 27:24 (NKJV): "saying, 'Do not be afraid, Paul; you must be brought before Caesar; and indeed God has granted you all those who sail with you.'"

Acts 27:25 (NKJV): "Therefore take heart, men, for I believe God that it will be just as it was told me."

The Word of Wisdom revealed to Ananias the plans and purpose of God, and the Word of Knowledge revealed specific facts to Ananias.

Acts 9:10 (KJV): "And there was a certain disciple at Damascus, named Ananias; and to him said the Lord in a vision, Ananias. And he said, Behold, I am here, Lord."

Acts 9:11 (KJV): "And the Lord said unto him, Arise, and go into the street which is called Straight, and enquire in the house of Judas for one called Saul, of Tarsus: for, behold, he prayeth,"

Acts 9:12 (KJV): "And hath seen in a vision a man named Ananias coming in, and putting his hand on him, that he might receive his sight."

Acts 9:13 (KJV): "Then Ananias answered, Lord, I have heard by many of this man, how much evil he hath done to thy saints at Jerusalem:"

Acts 9:14 (KJV): "And here he hath authority from the chief priests to bind all that call on thy name."

Acts 9:15 (KJV): "But the Lord said unto him, Go thy way: for he is a chosen vessel unto me, to bear my name before the Gentiles, and kings, and the children of Israel:"

Act 9:16 (KJV): "For I will shew him how great things he must suffer for my name's sake."

Word of Knowledge: A supernatural revelation given by the Spirit of God concerning certain facts in the mind of God about people, places, or things in the past or present (1 Cor. 12:8).

The Word of Knowledge will sometimes manifest through a vision, a dream, from an angel, or in conjunction with the Gift of Prophecy.

THE PURPOSE OF THE WORD OF KNOWLEDGE:

1. To bring supernatural encouragement

2. To give confirmation to what God has already been saying or doing

3. To provide insight, clarity, and direction related to God's plans and purpose, helping individuals or groups prepare for what God intends to do

4. To help with counseling and aid in evangelistic situations

5. To unlock hindrances to healing/unanswered prayers

6. To give strategies in spiritual warfare

7. To reveal where sin is being covered up

8. To open a meeting or situation for God to move

Old Testament Instances

Elisha Regarding the Syrians

Elisha was given a Word of Knowledge that revealed the plans (present) of the King of Syria.

2 Kings 6:8 (KJV): "Then the king of Syria warred against Israel, and took counsel with his servants, saying, 'In such and such a place shall be my camp.'"

2 Kings 6:9 (KJV): "And the man of God sent unto the king of Israel, saying, Beware that thou pass not such a place; for thither the Syrians are come down."

2 Kings 6:10 (KJV): "And the king of Israel sent to the place which the man of God told him and warned him of, and saved himself there, not once nor twice."

2 Kings 6:11 (KJV): "Therefore the heart of the king of Syria was sore troubled for this thing; and he called his servants, and said unto them, Will ye not shew me which of us is for the king of Israel?"

2 Kings 6:12 (KJV): "And one of his servants said, None, my lord, O king: but Elisha, the prophet that is in Israel, telleth the king of Israel the words that thou speakest in thy bedchamber."

New Testament Instances

Peter received a Word of Knowledge and Discernment concerning deception and greed on Ananias and Sapphira (Acts 5:1–11).

Acts 5:1 (KJV): "But a certain man named Ananias, with Sapphira his wife, sold a possession,"

Acts 5:2 (KJV): "And kept back part of the price, his wife also being privy to it, and brought a certain part, and laid it at the apostles' feet."

Acts 5:3 (KJV): "But Peter said, Ananias, why hath Satan filled thine heart to lie to the Holy Ghost, and to keep back part of the price of the land?"

Acts 5:4 (KJV): "Whiles it remained, was it not thine own? and after it was sold, was it not in thine own power? Why hast thou conceived this thing in thine heart? thou hast not lied unto men, but unto God.

The Word of Knowledge revealed to Ananias through a vision exact fact as to where to go, street name, the house and the name of the person to speak to (Acts 9:10–19).

Acts 9:10–12 (NKJV): "Now there was a certain disciple at Damascus named Ananias; and to him the Lord said in a vision, 'Ananias.'" And he said, "Here I am, Lord."

Acts 9:11 So the Lord said to him, "Arise and go to the street called Straight, and inquire at the house of Judas for one called Saul of Tarsus, for behold, he is praying.

Acts 9:12 "And in a vision, he has seen a man named Ananias coming in and putting his hand on him, so that he might receive his sight."

Discerning of Spirits:

This gives believers Supernatural insight into the spirit world, to discern both good and evil spirits (1 Corinthians 12:10).

Discerning of spirits is *seeing and hearing* into the spirit world.

It also reveals the kind of spirit at work behind a supernatural manifestation.

The biblical phrase "discerning of spirits" (1 Corinthians 12:10) is translated from the Greek words diakrisis pneumaton. *Diakrisis* is a compound word composed of two parts: *dia,* meaning "through," and krisis, meaning "to judge, divide, or distinguish." This refers to "one who judges or distinguishes through a situation to a decision."

Tim Blanchard teaches that *pneumaton* is the normal Greek word for "spirits." When combined with *diakrisis,* it refers to the process of judging through a person's speech and actions to discern the spirit behind them.

Different Classification of Spirits:

Holy Spirit	Angels	Demons or Evil spirits	Human spirits

This gift is not the following:

Discerning of character	Faults	Intentions

Old Testament Instances

Elijah Regarding Gehazi

Elisha demonstrates the gift of discerning spirits by perceiving Gehazi's actions and motives, thus exposing the spirit of greed, deceit, and lies.

2 Kings 5:21 (NIV): "So Gehazi hurried after Naaman. When Naaman saw him running toward him, he got down from the chariot to meet him. 'Is everything all right?' he asked."

2 Kings 21:22: "Everything is all right," Gehazi answered. "My master sent me to say, 'Two young men from the company of the prophets have just come to me from the hill country of Ephraim. Please give them a talent of silver and two sets of clothing.'"

2 Kings 21: 23 "By all means, take two talents," said Naaman. He urged Gehazi to accept them and then tied up the two talents of silver in two bags, with two sets of clothing. He gave them to two of his servants, and they carried them ahead of Gehazi.

2 Kings 21: 24 When Gehazi came to the hill, he took the things from the servants and put them away in the house. He sent the men away and they left.

2 Kings 21: 25 When he went in and stood before his master, Elisha asked him, "Where have you been, Gehazi?" "Your servant didn't go anywhere," Gehazi answered.

2 Kings 21: 26 But Elisha said to him, "Was not my spirit with you when the man got down from his chariot to meet you? Is this the time to take money or to accept clothes—or olive groves and vineyards, or flocks and herds, or male and female slaves?

2 Kings 21: 27 Naaman's leprosy will cling to you and to your descendants forever." Then Gehazi went from Elisha's presence, and his skin was leprous—it had become as white as snow.

New Testament Instances

DISCERNING OF THE HOLY SPIRIT

(1) John 1:32–33: "John the Baptist discerns the Holy Spirit upon Jesus as a dove."

Discerning of Angels:

(1) Luke 22:43: An angel appears to Jesus in the garden.

(2) John 20:11–13: Mary sees two angels in the sepulcher.

Discerning Human spirits:

(1) John 1:47: Jesus discerns a guileless spirit in Nathanael.

(2) Acts 14:8–10: Paul discerns a 'spirit of faith' in a lame man.

Discerning Evil spirits:

(1) Matt. 9:32–34: dumb spirit

(2) Matt. 12:22–24: spirit of blindness and dumbness

(3) Acts 16:16–18: Paul discerning slave girl spirit of divination (Python)

POWER GIFTS: THEY DO SOMETHING

The Gift of Faith is a supernatural manifestation of the Holy Spirit whereby a believer is empowered with supernatural faith (1 Cor. 12:9).

The Gift of Faith enables a person to receive a miracle beyond the capacity of ordinary faith.

The Gift of Faith is distinct from the other power gifts in that it involves a divine impartation of confidence, assurance, and unwavering trust that God will bring about a specific result. This supernatural faith goes beyond natural belief or general faith, allowing the recipient to believe in God for the impossible.

Three Types of Faith Referred to in the New Testament:

1. Saving or General Faith: Eph. 2:8; Rom. 12:3; Rom. 10:17

2. Fruit of the Spirit—Faith or Faithfulness: Gal. 5:22

3. Gift of Faith -1Cor. 12:9

Characteristics of the Gift of Faith

» The Gift of Faith is passive.

» The Gift of Faith receives a miracle.

Instances of the Gift of Faith in Operation:
Jesus raised Lazarus from the dead.

In this instance, all three Power Gifts were in operation.

John 11:39–44 (KJV): "And he that was dead came forth, bound hand and foot with grave clothes: and his face was bound about with a napkin. Jesus saith unto them, loose him, and let him go."

The Gift of Faith Was Actively at Work, Providing Protection in Moments of Danger:
Paul received divine protection and safety for himself and everyone on board in (Acts 27:1–44).

Daniel received divine protection from the lions. (He passively received his miracle, Daniel 6:21–23).

ELIJAH RECEIVED SUPERNATURAL PROVISION DURING FAMINE

1 Kings 17:2–6

(1) **1 Kings 17:2 (NIV):** "Then the word of the Lord came to Elijah:"

(2) "Leave here, turn eastward and hide in the Kerith Ravine, east of the Jordan."

(3) "You will drink from the brook, and I have directed the ravens to supply you with food there."

(4) "So he did what the Lord had told him. He went to the Kerith Ravine, east of the Jordan, and stayed there."

(5) "The ravens brought him bread and meat in the morning and bread and meat in the evening, and he drank from the brook."

Working of Miracles:

The supernatural Gift given by God to work a Miracle, thus intervening in the natural course of nature.

1 Cor. 12:10 (NKJV): "to another the working of miracles, to another prophecy, to another discerning of spirits, to another different kinds of tongues, to another the interpretation of tongues."

A Miracle is a supernatural intervention by God in the ordinary course of nature, a temporary suspension of the accustomed order, or interruption in the system of nature as we know it, operated by the power of the Holy Spirit.

> » The Greek word for miracle is dunamis and can be translated as "acts of power" (1 Cor. 12:10).
>
> » This Gift actively works a miracle.

Instances of the Working of Miracles in Operation:

(1)   Loaves were multiplied: Matthew 14:17–21; Mark 6:38–44; Luke 9:13–17

(2)   A multitude of fish filled the Disciples' net: John 21:8, 11

(3)   Widow's pot of oil never ran out: 2 Kings 4:1–7

(4)   Turning water into wine: John 2:1–11

Gifts of Healings:

The Gifts of Healings operate supernaturally to bring health and restoration beyond what is naturally possible (1 Cor. 12:9).

Key Facts:

> » The purpose of this gift is to heal the sick and to destroy the work of the devil in the human body.
>
> » Healing can manifest over a period of time as well as immediately.
>
> » Not all healing results from the Gifts of Healing in operation.

In (Mark 11:23–24), healing can occur by operating in faith. Although the healing is supernatural, it's not the Gift of Healing in operation.

Instances of the Gifts of Healings in Operation:
Peter and John operate in the Gift of Healing at the gate of the temple. Peter heals a lame beggar (Acts 3:1–9).

Jesus healed numerous people during his Ministry. Matt. 8:14–17, 15:29–31, 12:22

PAUL HEALED MANY ON THE ISLAND OF MALTA

Act 28:7 (KJV): "In the same quarters were possessions of the chief man of the island, whose name was Publius; who received us, and lodged us three days courteously."

Act 28:8 (KJV): "And it came to pass, that the father of Publius lay sick of a fever and of a bloody flux: to whom Paul entered in, and prayed, and laid his hands on him, and healed him."

Act 28:9 (KJV): "So when this was done, others also, which had diseases in the island, came, and were healed:"

INSPIRATIONAL GIFTS/VOCAL GIFTS: THEY SAY SOMETHING

Gift of Prophecy: It is an inspired word given by the Holy Spirit to an individual to communicate God's thoughts and intentions to mankind. Speaking unto men for edification, exhortation, and comfort (1 Cor. 12:10).

Prophesy (Hebrew): *Naba* (nawbaw) means to prophesy, speak, or sing by inspiration. It conveys the sense of bubbling forth or flowing forth—like a fountain. It also carries the thought of letting drop, lifting up, springing forth, and releasing divine utterance.

Naba, as taken from the Hebrew, can be experienced in worship, praise, intercession, corporate prayer, singing, preaching, and teaching.

Prophesy (Greek): The Greek word for prophecy, *propheteia,* implies speaking for another—specifically, speaking on behalf of God.

1 Corinthians 14:1 (KJV): "Follow after charity, and desire spiritual gifts, but rather that ye may prophesy."

1 Corinthians 14:2: "For he that speaketh in an unknown tongue speaketh not unto men, but unto God: for no man understandeth him; howbeit in the spirit he speaketh mysteries."

1 Corinthians 14:3: "But he that prophesieth speaketh unto men to edification, and exhortation, and comfort."

1 Corinthians 14:4: "He that speaketh in an unknown tongue edifieth himself; but he that prophesieth edifieth the church."

1 Corinthians 14:5: "I would that ye all spake with tongues, but rather that ye prophesied: for greater is he that prophesieth than he that speaketh with tongues, except he interpret, that the church may receive edifying."

1 Corinthians 14:39 (KJV): "Wherefore, brethren, covet to prophesy, and forbid not to speak with tongues."

Romans 12:6 (KJV): "Having then gifts differing according to the grace that is given to us, whether prophecy, let us prophesy according to the proportion of faith:"

1 Corinthians 13:2 (KJV): "And though I have the gift of prophecy…"

1 Corinthians 12:31 (KJV): "But covet earnestly the best gift…"

The Gift of Prophecy

> » It is for edification, exhortation, and comfort.
>
> » There is no revelation expressed with this gift.
>
> » There is no foretelling or prediction.

TWO TYPES OF PROPHECIES:

Unconditional Prophecies:
Don't depend upon any assistance for fulfillment. These prophecies are typically found in a covenant structure, such as the covenant with Abraham (Gen 15).

Conditional Prophecies:
Based on the obedience or disobedience to God's Word. There is usually an "if" or "unless" attached to it (Jer. 18:7–10). Oftentimes, this is corporate; however, it may apply to individuals as well.

Gift of Tongues:
A supernatural utterance by the Holy Spirit in languages never learned by the speaker, nor understood by the hearer (1 Cor. 12:10).

TWO KINDS OF TONGUES:

Personal Prayer Language (Devotional Tongues):
Used in private prayer and worship. These tongues are for personal edification and communion with God. Interpretation is not required, as the focus is intimacy, not instruction (1 Corinthians 14:2, Romans 8:26).

The Gift of Tongues:
Intended for public ministry and corporate gatherings. This gift delivers a message that must be interpreted to benefit others (see 1 Corinthians 12:10, 14:27–28). Often prophetic in nature, it functions alongside the gift of interpretation.

Personal Prayer Language

Purpose:

Edifies himself: 1 Corinthians 14:4 (KJV): "He that speaketh in an unknown tongue edifieth himself; but he that prophesieth edifieth the church."

Building yourselves up: Jude 1:20 (KJV): "But ye, beloved, building up yourselves on your most holy faith, praying in the Holy Ghost,

Act of your personal will: 1 Corinthians 14:15 (KJV): "What is it then? I will pray with the spirit, and I will pray with the understanding also: I will sing with the spirit, and I will sing with the understanding also."

All can pray in tongues at one time: Acts 2:4 (KJV): "And they were all filled with the Holy Ghost, and began to speak with other tongues, as the Spirit gave them utterance."

No interpretation is necessary. However, there are instances in which you may receive an understanding of your prayer language.

Tongues and Interpretation

Gift of Tongues Edifies the Body of Christ:

1 Corinthians 14:5 (KJV): "I would that ye all spake with tongues, but rather that ye prophesied: for greater is he that prophesieth than he that speaketh with tongues, except he interpret, that the church may receive edifying."

As the Holy Spirit Will:

1 Corinthians 12:11 (KJV): "But all these worketh that one and the selfsame Spirit, dividing to every man severally as he will."

1 Corinthians 14:27 (KJV): "If any man speak in an unknown tongue, let it be by two, or at the most by three, and that by course; and let one interpret."

Interpretation Is Necessary!

Interpretation of Tongues:

The supernatural manifestation of the Holy Spirit using one's vocal organs, giving the meaning of an utterance in other tongues (1 Cor. 12:10).

Interpretation (Strong's 2058 *hermēneía*): giving the gist of a message rather than a strict translation. It conveys an equivalent meaning, not a word-for-word rendering.

This *Gift* operates in conjunction with *The Gift of Tongues*.

In other words, this is interpretation, not translation!

CHAPTER 3 EXERCISE

ACTIVATION EXERCISE: ALLOW 20 MINUTES PER EXERCISE.

Purpose: *to assist students in understanding and recognizing their spiritual gifts*

Word of Knowledge

Have students pair off into groups of two. Ask students to pray in the Spirit for two to three minutes. Quiet themselves for one to two minutes while focusing on the other person. Ask God for a specific word or phrase to share with the other person.

Remember, a Word of Knowledge deals with the past and present. This can be anything (for example, a number, a single word, a sentence, or even a song). In a second step, ask God what He wants to tell the other person through it.

Purpose: *This exercise is designed to help students remain sensitive to the multiple channels in which God speaks.*

Prophetic words don't only reveal the future; they can also interpret the past and give understanding for the present.

*Choose one of these three and let everyone ask God for a word for another person about their **past, present, or future.** Example: "God, what moved your heart about the childhood of person xyz?" or "God, is there anything you want to tell this person about their current situation/circumstances?"*

Gifts of the Holy Spirit
Chapter 3 Worksheet

Purpose: to gain insight, understanding, and revelation to be able to accurately identify and function in the grace gifting that's upon your life

1. List the Nine Spiritual Gifts

__________________________ , __________________________

__________________________ , __________________________

__________________________ , __________________________

__________________________ , __________________________

__________________________ .

2. What is the overall purpose of spiritual gifts? Give a scriptural reference.

____

____

____

____

____

____

3. List the three categories of gifts and how they function.

__________________________ , __________________________

__________________________ .

4. Who is the giver of the gifts?

____

____

____

____

____

5. Define Word of Wisdom.

____

____

____

____

____

6. Name an instance in the Bible where the word of wisdom was in operation (not listed in your study).

____

____

____

____

7. Define "Word of Knowledge."

____

____

____

____

8. Define "Discerning of Spirits."

____

____

____

____

9. Can you operate in the Gift of Faith at any given time? If so, please explain.

____

____

____

____

10. Define "Working of Miracles."

____

____

____

____

11. Give an example of the Working of Miracles in operation.

____

____

____

____

12. Define "Gift of Healing."

____

____

____

____

13. What is the purpose of the Gift of Healing in operation?

____

____

____

____

14. What is the purpose of the gift of prophecy in manifestation?

____

____

____

____

15. Define "Divers Kinds of Tongues."

____

____

____

____

____

16. Is this the same as your prayer Language? Why or why not? Support with a scripture reference.

____

____

____

____

____

17. Define the Interpretation of Tongues.

____

____

____

____

18. If there is no interpreter, should a message be given in tongues? Why or why not? Support with a scripture reference.

____

____

____

____

19. Which of these gifts have you been able to identify in your life?

____

____

____

____

20. Which gifts do you operate in most frequently?

Notes:

CHAPTER 04
FIVEFOLD MINISTRY GIFTS

Eph 4:11–13(NIV): "So Christ himself gave the apostles, the prophets, the evangelists, the pastors and teachers,"

(12) "to equip his people for works of service, so that the body of Christ may be built up,"

(13) "until we all reach unity in the faith and in the knowledge of the Son of God and become mature, attaining to the whole measure of the fullness of Christ."

THE GIFT GIVER: JESUS

These are ascension *Gifts* given by Jesus.

Ephesians 4:8: "Wherefore he saith, when he ascended up on high, he led captivity captive, and gave gifts unto men."

Gifts is doma (Greek, Strong's #1390), which comes from the root word didomi, which means "to give."

WHO ARE THE GIFTS?

Ephesians 4:11 (KJV): "And he gave some, apostles; and some, prophets; and some, evangelists; and some, pastors and teachers."

Purpose of the Gifts:
Ephesians 4:12 (KJV): "For the perfecting of the saints, for the work of the ministry, for the edifying of the body of Christ:

> » For the perfecting (spiritual maturity) of the saints
>
> » For the work of the ministry (to teach)
>
> » For the edifying (building up) of the body of Christ

How Long Will the Gifts Function?
Ephesians 4:13 (KJV): "Till we all come in the unity of the faith, and of the knowledge of the Son of God, unto a perfect man, unto the measure of the stature of the fullness of Christ:"

> » Till the body of Christ comes into unity of the faith
>
> » Until the body of Christ reaches maturity
>
> » Till we measure up to the standards of Christ

Apostle

The Greek word *apostolos* translates as "one sent forth."

Jim Goll (2001) defines an apostle as "one called and sent by Christ to have the spiritual authority, character, gifts, and abilities to reach and establish people in Kingdom truth and order, especially through founding and overseeing local churches."

Apostle is listed seventy-eight times and *messenger* twice in the Bible. Messenger is translated from the same Greek word, *apostolos*.

Characteristics of an Apostle:

> » Apostles are visionary and globally minded (2 Cor. 8).
>
> » They are patient and long-suffering (Gal. 5:22–23).
>
> » They are multifaceted and strong in administration.
>
> » Apostle has the grace to function in all nine Gifts of the Holy Spirit (1 Cor. 12:8–11)!

» They establish the spiritual foundation of new local churches (1 Cor. 3:10).

» The Apostle grounds the church in biblical truths(1 Cor. 1:23).

» Apostles are pioneers. They blaze trails for others to follow (1 Corinthians 3:6).

» The Apostles establish the church through solid biblical teaching (Acts 11:25–26).

» The Apostle has governmental oversight of a church until it's established.

» They are graced to build churches and establish ministries.

» Apostles are graced to build, train, mentor, and equip people 1 Cor. 3:10).

» Apostles set things in order (Titus 1:5).

» Apostles have the authority to appoint elders, leaders, and positions of authority (Titus 1:5).

» They operate in signs, wonders, and miracles (2 Cor. 12:12).

Wisdom Nugget: That which we need the most is that which we understand the least!

Biblical Examples of Apostles:

- **Jesus Christ,** the chief apostle (Hebrews 3:1)
- **Barnabas and Paul** (Acts 13:2, 4, 14:14)
- **The Twelve Apostles** (Luke 6:13)
- **James, the Lord's brother** (Galatians 1:19)
- **Andronicus and Junia** (Romans 16:7)
- **Matthias** (Acts 1:26)
- **James** (Galatians 1:19; 1 Corinthians 15:7)
- Two unnamed "apostles of the churches" (2 Corinthians 8:23)
- **Timothy and Sylvanus/Silas** (1 Thessalonians 1:1, 2:6)
- **Epaphroditus** (Philippians 2:25)
- **Apollos** (1 Corinthians 4:4–9)

Prophet

Prophet (Greek, *prophḗtēs,* Strong's #4396) refers to one who declares the mind—or message—of God.

This sometimes includes *foretelling* (predicting future events), but more often involves *forth-telling*—speaking God's message into a specific situation.

The word prophḗtēs is a transliteration of the compound Greek word pro ("for, on behalf of") and phēmi ("to speak"), meaning "to speak for another."

Prophets proclaim a divine message and speak on behalf of God. They reveal a fragment of His mind to a person or group concerning past, present, or future events.

FOUR HEBREW WORDS TRANSLATED "PROPHET"

1. Nabi/Naba (Hebrew, Strong's #5030)

One who speaks for God: "to bubble forth" like a fountain; to gush, pour, or chant. This word describes one who announces or pours forth the declarations of God.

» Used 424 times in the Old Testament.

2. Roeh—Seer (Hebrew, Strong's #7203)

Refers to the divine ability to perceive on multiple levels into the unseen realm—past, present, or future—and to reveal the mind of God.

Two Hebrew Words Translated "Seer":

» Roeh—vision; a seer (1 Samuel 9:11)

» Chozeh (Hebrew, Strong's #2374): one who receives communication from God; one who sees (2 Samuel 24:11)

3. Nataph (Hebrew, Strong's #5197)

"To prophesy," "to drop," or "to fall as drops of rain." This word describes another aspect of prophetic ministry—gentle, timely, and Spirit-led (Micah 2:6–7).

4. Shamar (Hebrew, Strong's #8104)

Shamar is a Hebrew word meaning "prophet" as a watchman—one who guards, protects, and keeps. It means "to hedge about as with thorns," "to guard," "to protect," "to keep," and "to be a watchman." This word can refer to guarding a flock, the heart, the mind, a nation, or a city from outside attack or ungodly influences. It's also used to refer to keeping (guarding) the gates or entrances to cities.

When setting someone free from captivity, you begin to stir up gifts, heal, restore, and mobilize people into the office they're called to occupy.

Shamar gives prophets the status of spiritual guards, warriors, supernatural enforcers, and keepers of the churches of God (Jeremiah 17:16, 50:6–7).

CHARACTERISTICS OF A PROPHET: A PROPHET'S GUIDE

» Prophets are intercessors, but not all intercessors are prophets.

» A Prophet's life is a prophetic message or model of what is to come. Old Testament prophets modeled this for Israel, for example, Hosea.

» Prophets impart, motivate, and stir up the gifts of God (2 Tim. 1:6).

» Prophets are often spontaneous, quick, and zealous.

» Prophets are Foundational Ministry Gifts (Ephesians 3:5).

» Prophets are principle-centered; they often see things as black or white, no gray area.

» Prophets can be critical and judgmental in their thinking.

FUNCTION OF A PROPHET

» Prophets reveal God's heart to His people.

» Prophets provide guidance to individuals and the broader body of Christ.

» They provide revelation, as well as interpretation, application, and guidance on timing.

» Prophets provide prayer coverage and counsel. They can see what's coming and provide direction.

» The Gift of prophecy and all three revelatory gifts are characteristic of the prophetic office. They must prove to manifest consistently for one to qualify as a prophet (1 Cor. 12:10).

» Prophets Release Warnings and Judgment: 1 Timothy 1:20; 1 Corinthians 5:5

» Prophets release warnings and judgment as part of their divine assignment.

» In 1 Timothy 1:20, Paul speaks of Hymenaeus and Alexander being "handed over to Satan" so they may learn not to blaspheme.

» In 1 Corinthians 5:5, Paul instructs the church to "deliver such a one to Satan for the destruction of the flesh, that his Spirit may be saved."

» Prophets provide insight and direction (Acts 13:1–3).

» Prophets confer and impart: 1 Timothy 4:14; 2 Tim. 1:6; Rom. 1:11

» Prophets give confirmation of the will of God: 2 Corinthians 13:1; Acts 15:32

» Prophets bring correction (1 Cor. 14:31).

» Prophets foretell future events to help prepare the church in advance (Acts 11:27–30).

» Prophets may reveal (not call) a person to the fivefold ministry and lay hands upon them to anoint them.

» Prophets sound the alarm in times of transition, judgment, expansion, and warfare.

» Prophets hear from God in unique ways to bring clarity and perspective to the Church in difficult times.

» Prophets are used to awaken and activate the body to the purpose of God for their time.

EXAMPLES OF OLD AND NEW TESTAMENT PROPHETS:

» Abraham	» Jonah, Hosea, Amos, Micah, Nahum
» Moses	» Zephaniah, Habakkuk, Haggai, Zechariah, Malachi
» Samuel	» Jesus
» Elijah	» Paul
» Elisha,	» Agabus (Acts 21:10)
» Isaiah, Jeremiah, Ezekiel, Daniel, Obadiah, Joel	» Judas and Silas (Acts 15:32)
	» Anna

Evangelist

Evangelist (Greek, Strong's #2099)

The Greek word euangelistēs means "a messenger of good" or "preacher of the gospel." It's a compound word formed from eu ("well") and *angelos* ("messenger"): literally, "a messenger of good news."

This word appears only three times in Scripture:

CHARACTERISTICS OF AN EVANGELIST: EVANGELIST GATHER

» Evangelists have a burning desire to reach the lost and win them to Christ.

» Evangelists stir up gifts, encourage, and want to be part of the revival.

» They make disciples and witnesses for Jesus Christ.

» An Evangelist ministry is characterized by the Power Gifts in operation (1 Cor. 12:9–10).

» Evangelists are bold and aggressive in their delivery and mannerisms.

» They are usually transient; however, they will be submitted to a local church for oversight and guidance.

» They are called outside of the church walls to reach the lost.

» They emphasize outreaches and witnessing in the local assembly.

» They preach a simple message of salvation.

FUNCTION OF AN EVANGELIST

» Evangelists carry a significant burden for those who are not a part of the kingdom of God.

» They carry an anointing to preach the gospel with great conviction and draw people to the Lord.

» Signs, wonders, and miracles are the emphasis of their ministry.

» Evangelists preach Christ (Acts 8:12).

» Evangelists train and develop believers to win souls.

EXAMPLES OF EVANGELISTS

» Philip (Acts 8:26–40)

» Paul instructs Timothy to "do the work of an evangelist" (2 Timothy 4:5). He was never called an Evangelist … so we can do the work of an Evangelist without being one.

Pastor

Pastor (Greek, Strong's #4166)

The Greek word *poimēn* means "shepherd"—one who tends the sheep or cares for flocks.

The word pastor is used once in Scripture (Ephesians 4:11) to describe one of the five ministry gifts given to the church.

Jesus referred to Himself as the good shepherd (John 10:11).

John 10:11: "I am the good shepherd: the good shepherd giveth his life for the sheep."

- » Pastors have a heart of compassion and are long-suffering.

- » They are men and women after God's heart.

- » Loves fellowship and invests individual time with the flock.

- » Pastors are relational and love networking.

- » Pastors are nurturers by nature.

FUNCTION OF THE PASTOR:

- » The pastor has a heart for the church.

- » He cares for and nurtures his sheep.

- » He feeds and leads the flock.

- » His passion is to see the flock grow and mature.

- » Pastors have an anointing that draws the distressed, abused, rejected, neglected, and the unlovable.

- » He gathers the flock together in unity.

- » Pastors guard and shepherd the flock (Acts 20:28–30).

- » A pastor's ministry is characterized by these Gifts in operation:

  - The word of knowledge

  - The word of wisdom (Revelatory Gifts)

  - Tongues and interpretation of tongues (Inspirational gifts)

Teacher

Teacher (Greek, Strong's #1320)

The Greek word didaskalos comes from *didaskō,* meaning "to give instruction."

It refers to one who teaches—a communicator of truth, clarity, and spiritual understanding.

Jesus was the *Master Teacher,* revealing the heart of the Father through parables, doctrine, and daily example.

In Acts 13:1–2, Luke mentions four men recognized as *prophets* and teachers— functioning in *both offices* as they ministered to the Lord and fasted.

Acts 13:1–2: Prophets and Teachers at Antioch

Now there were certain prophets and teachers in the church at Antioch: Barnabas, Simeon called Niger, Lucius of Cyrene, Manaen (who had been brought up with Herod the tetrarch), and Saul.

As they ministered to the Lord and fasted, the Holy Ghost said, "Separate unto Me Barnabas and Saul for the work whereunto I have called them."

CHARACTERISTICS OF A TEACHER: TEACHERS GROUND THE BODY

» Teachers have a passion for studying the Word.

» They love to dig beneath the surface of the Word of God.

» Teachers are usually itinerant ministers unless they also possess the pastoral gift.

FUNCTIONS OF A TEACHER:

- Teachers teach line upon line, precept upon precept (Isaiah 28:9, 10).

- Teachers impart divine life and revelation.

- Teachers illuminate Scripture and bring forth spiritual truth.

- Teachers teach the fundamental principles of the Word.

EXAMPLES OF TEACHERS:

Acts 13:1 (NKJV): "Now there were in the church that was at Antioch certain prophets and teachers; as Barnabas, and Simeon that was called Niger, and Lucius of Cyrene, and Manaen, which had been brought up with Herod the tetrarch, and Saul."

» Barnabas (Acts 11:22–26)

» Simeon

» Lucius

» Manaen

CHAPTER 4 EXERCISE

ACTIVATION EXERCISE: ALLOW 20 MINUTES FOR PROPHETIC EXERCISE.

Purpose: *This activation challenges students to release their faith to minister to a large group of believers, preparing them for corporate ministry rather than just individual or small group settings.*

Instructor: *Select four students whom you feel are more mature in the spirit for this exercise. Bring them before the class. Ask them, along with the class, to begin praying in the Spirit for two minutes.*

Be silent for about 45–60 seconds. Now focus on what you see, what pictures are forming in your mind's eye? What do you "hear" in your Spirit? What do you sense in your "knower"? Ask them to release what they see (if necessary, describe the picture), hear, or sense. Allow each student an opportunity to share their thoughts.

Ministry Gifts
Chapter 4 Worksheet

Purpose: to give insight, revelation, and understanding of the purpose, characteristics, and function of the various ministry gifts

1. According to Ephesians 4:11, 12, who gave the gifts and for what purpose?

____

____

____

____

____

____

2. Why are they called ascension gifts?

____

____

____

____

____

____

3. List the three categories of gifts and how they function.

_____________________________, ___________________________

_____________________________, ___________________________

_____________________________.

4. What is the definition of an Apostle?

____

____

____

____

____

5. List three characteristics of an Apostle.

a) ____

b) ____

c) ____

6. Name four ways in which an Apostle functions.

a) ____

b) ____

c) ____

d) ____

7. What is the Greek word for *prophet*?

____

8. Define *prophet*.

____

____

____

____

____

9. Name two types of prophets and define them.

a) ____

____

____

____

b) ____

____

____

____

10. A prophet operates in which spiritual gifts?

_______________________ , _______________________

_______________________ , _______________________ .

11. According to 1 Cor. 14:31, a prophet brings_______________________ .

12. A *prophet* is a_______________________ Ministry Gift according to Eph. 3:5.

13. Name three characteristics of a prophet.

    a) _______________________

    b) _______________________

    c) _______________________

14. List five prophets in the Bible

_______________________ , _______________________

_______________________ , _______________________

_______________________ .

15. Define Evangelist.

____

____

____

____

____

____

16. What is the heart of an Evangelist?

____

____

____

____

____

____

17. What gifts characterize the Evangelist ministry?

______________________, ______________________

______________________, ______________________

______________________.

18. How does an Evangelist function?

____

____

____

____

____

____

19. According to John 10:11, who was the good shepherd?______________

20. How many times was the word "pastor" used in scripture, and where?

____

____

21. List three characteristics of a pastor.

    a) ____

    b) ____

    c) ____

22. According to Acts 20:28–30, what is the responsibility of the pastor?

____

____

____

____

____

The pastor's office is characterized by which spiritual gifts?

______________________, ______________________

______________________, ______________________.

24. Define *teacher.*

____

25. What is a teacher's main emphasis?

____

26. Name two ways in which a teacher functions in the Body.

   a) ____

   b) ____

27. Name three teachers in the Bible.

   a) ____

   b) ____

   c) ____

Notes:

CHAPTER 05

FIVE METHODS OF PROPHESYING

Romans 12:6 (KJV): "Having then gifts differing according to the grace that is given to us, whether prophecy, let us prophesy according to the proportion of faith;"

Prophesy in proportion to the measure of the grace gifting upon your life.

1 Corinthians 14:31 (KJV): "For ye may all prophesy one by one, that all may learn, and all may be comforted."

There are five distinct prophetic methods that God uses to minister to His body:

The Spirit of Prophecy | Gift of Prophecy | Prophetic Presbytery

Prophetic Preaching | The Office of the Prophet (discussed in Chapter 4)

The Spirit of Prophecy

WHAT IS THE SPIRIT OF PROPHECY?

The Spirit of Prophecy is an anointing. It is God's manifested presence and anointing that oftentimes manifests in a corporate gathering to speak forth the mind and will of God as the Holy Spirit wills.

92

The Spirit of Prophecy Is the Testimony of Jesus

Revelation 19:10 (NKJV): "And I fell at his feet to worship him. But he said to me, "See that you do not do that! I am your fellow servant, and of your brethren who have the testimony of Jesus. Worship God! For the testimony of Jesus is the spirit of prophecy."

The Spirit of prophecy is not an office or a gift. It can't be earned or received by prayer and fasting.

The Spirit of Prophecy Can Be Expressed Through Various Methods:

- » A word from the Lord

- » Prophetic presbytery

- » The song of the Lord; prophetic song

- » Worship through dance

When the Spirit of Prophecy is in manifestation, anyone who has the desire and faith can prophesy. You don't have to have the Gift of Prophecy or be a Prophet.

Romans 12:6 (KJV): "Having then gifts differing according to the grace that is given to us, whether prophecy, let us prophesy according to the proportion of faith;"

- » The Spirit of Prophecy often manifests in a strong atmosphere of prophetic worship.

- » The Spirit of Prophecy flows when there is a company of Prophets and the atmosphere has been prophetically charged.

- » The Spirit of Prophecy usually manifests in a corporate setting.

Examples of the Spirit of Prophecy in Manifestation

Saul met a company of prophets, and the spirit of prophecy came on him, and he began to prophesy. Saul wasn't a prophet. He was anointed King.

1 Samuel 10:10 (KJV): "And when they came thither to the hill, behold, a company of prophets met him; and the Spirit of God came upon him, and he prophesied among them."

1 Samuel 10:11 (KJV): "And it came to pass, when all that knew him beforetime saw that, behold, he prophesied among the prophets, then the people said one to another, What is this that is come unto the son of Kish? Is Saul also among the prophets?"

The Spirit of the Lord came on Saul's messengers, and they began to prophesy.

1 Samuel 19:20 (KJV): "And Saul sent messengers to take David: and when they saw the company of the prophets prophesying, and Samuel standing as appointed over them, the Spirit of God was upon the messengers of Saul, and they also prophesied."

1 Samuel 19:21 (KJV): "And when it was told Saul, he sent other messengers, and they prophesied likewise. And Saul sent messengers again the third time, and they prophesied also."

1 Samuel 19:22 (KJV): "Then he also went to Ramah, and came to a great well that is in Sechu: and he asked and said, Where are Samuel and David? And one said, Behold, they be at Naioth in Ramah."

1 Samuel 19:23 (KJV): "And he went thither to Naioth in Ramah: and the Spirit of God was upon him also, and he went on, and prophesied, until he came to Naioth in Ramah."

1 Samuel 19:24 (KJV): "And he stripped off his clothes also, and prophesied before Samuel in like manner, and lay down naked all that day and all that night. Wherefore they say, Is Saul also among the prophets?"

During a corporate gathering, the Spirit of the Lord came upon Jahaziel, and he began to prophesy.

2 Chronicles 20:12–(KJV): "O our God, wilt thou not judge them? for we have no might against this great company that cometh against us; neither know we what to do: but our eyes are upon thee."

2 Chronicles 20:13 (KJV): "And all Judah stood before the LORD, with their little ones, their wives, and their children."

2 Chronicles 20:14 (KJV): "Then upon Jahaziel the son of Zechariah, the son of Benaiah, the son of Jeiel, the son of Mattaniah, a Levite of the sons of Asaph, came the Spirit of the LORD in the midst of the congregation;"

2 Chronicles 20:15 (KJV): "And he said, Hearken ye, all Judah, and ye inhabitants of Jerusalem, and thou king Jehoshaphat, Thus saith the LORD unto you, Be not afraid nor dismayed by reason of this great multitude; for the battle is not yours, but God's."

2 Chronicles 20:16 (KJV): "Tomorrow go ye down against them: behold, they come up by the cliff of Ziz; and ye shall find them at the end of the brook, before the wilderness of Jeruel."

2 Chronicles 20:17 (KJV): "Ye shall not need to fight in this battle: set yourselves, stand ye still, and see the salvation of the LORD with you, O Judah and Jerusalem: fear not, nor be dismayed; tomorrow go out against them: for the LORD will be with you."

Moses gathered the seventy, and God took of the spirit that was upon Moses and released it upon the seventy.

Numbers 11:24 (KJV): "And Moses went out, and told the people the words of the LORD, and gathered the seventy men of the elders of the people, and set them round about the tabernacle."

Numbers 11:25 (KJV): "And the LORD came down in a cloud, and spake unto him, and took of the spirit that was upon him, and gave it unto the seventy elders: and it came to pass, that, when the spirit rested upon them, they prophesied, and did not cease."

Numbers 11:26 (KJV): "But there remained two of the men in the camp, the name of the one was Eldad, and the name of the other Medad: and the spirit rested upon them; and they were of them that were written, but went not out unto the tabernacle: and they prophesied in the camp."

Numbers 11:27 (KJV): "And there ran a young man, and told Moses, and said, Eldad and Medad do prophesy in the camp."

Numbers 11:28 (KJV): "And Joshua the son of Nun, the servant of Moses, one of his young men, answered and said, My lord Moses, forbid them."

Numbers 11:29 (KJV): "And Moses said unto him, Enviest thou for my sake? would God that all the LORD'S people were prophets, and that the LORD would put his spirit upon them!

The Gift of Prophecy

1 Corinthians 14:1 (KJV): "Follow after charity, and desire spiritual gifts, but rather that ye may prophesy."

1 Corinthians 12:31 (KJV): "But covet earnestly the best gifts: and yet shew I unto you a more excellent way.

Paul exhorts us to desire spiritual gifts, especially the gift of prophecy. Why?

Purpose:

» It edifies (builds up) the Church (1 Corinthians 14:4).

» Prophecy is a sign for believers (1 Corinthians 14:22).

» Prophecy has the potential to bless multitudes at a time.

Gift of Prophecy: It is an inspired word given by the Holy Spirit to an individual to communicate God's thoughts and intentions to mankind. It is speaking unto men for edification, exhortation, and comfort.

Prophesy (Hebrew: *naba [nawbaw]*) means to prophesy—to speak or sing by inspiration. It conveys the sense of bubbling forth or flowing out. The imagery includes bubbling up like a fountain, letting drop, flowing forth, lifting up, and springing forth.

The experience of *naba*—as drawn from the Hebrew—can manifest through *worship, praise, intercession, corporate prayer, singing, preaching, and teaching.*

Prophesy (Greek) means to speak for another.

The Gift of Prophecy is one of the nine gifts of the Holy Spirit.

1 Corinthians 12:10 (KJV): "To another the working of miracles; to another prophecy; to another discerning of spirits; to another divers kinds of tongues; to another the interpretation of tongues:"

96

» Gift of Prophecy is for edification, exhortation, and comfort.

1 Corinthians 14:3 (KJV): "But he that prophesieth speaketh unto men to edification, and exhortation, and comfort."

Gift of Prophecy can operate in various forms:

- » The spoken (verbal) word

- » The written word

- » Song of the Lord; 2 Kings 3:15, Colossians 3:16

- » Dance and expressive movement

- » Musical instruments (Instruments may prophesy through sound.) David played a harp to drive the evil spirit away from King Saul   (1 Samuel 16:14–23; 1 Samuel 18:10; 1 Samuel 19:9).

1 Chronicles 25:1 (NIV): "David, together with the commanders of the army, set apart some of the sons of Asaph, Heman, and Jeduthun for the ministry of prophesying, accompanied by harps, lyres, and cymbals. Here is the list of the men who performed this service:"

Prophetic Presbytery: A Team-Based Ministry

Prophetic Presbytery is when two or more prophets and/or prophetic ministers lay hands on and prophesy over individuals at a specified time and place (as described by Prophet Lauro R. Adame).

This is the team concept of ministering prophetically to individuals or groups.

The word *presbytery* comes from the Greek word *presbyteros,* meaning "elder" (i.e., a church leader).

The Greek word *presbytery (presbeterion)* means an order, a council of elders, or the celestial council of heaven (Strong's 4244).

From the word presbuteros, meaning: an elder, presbyter, or a council member of the celestial council.

The word elder comes from the Greek *episkopos,* meaning "overseer" or "to supervise."

Another word for elder is bishop, which came from the Greek *episkopos* to *piskop,* and eventually to *bishop.*

Purposes and Functions of Prophetic Presbyteries:

1. To reveal, activate, and confirm a church member's membership in the Body of Christ

2. To minister a rhema word of God to individuals who are in major transitions in their lives

3. To release the impartation and activation of divinely ordained gifts, graces, and callings

4. To release revelation, clarification, and confirmation of leadership ministry in the church

5. To lay hands on and prophecy over those called, and to be ordained as a fivefold minister (Titus 1:5)

EXAMPLES OF PROPHETIC PRESBYTERY:

» Jeremiah's conflict with Hananiah in Jeremiah 28 further reinforces this as the king summoned an apparent presbytery of prophets to advise him on an impending military campaign.

» A similar example is seen in 1 Kings 22 with Ahab and Micaiah.

» Paul speaks of a prophesying presbytery in 1 Timothy 4:14: (KJV): "Neglect not the gift that is in thee, which was given thee by prophecy, with the laying on of the hands of the presbytery."

Prophetic Preaching

Prophetic preaching is spontaneous revelation received from the Holy Spirit, quickening one to speak forth the mind, will, and counsel of God, of things that have not been studied.

1. Prophetic preaching is a divine unction from the Holy Spirit to declare a new word from the Lord.

2. Prophetic preaching is revelatory and spontaneous. (It's not a rehearsed sermon.)

3. All fivefold ministers may operate in this function.

4. Prophetic preaching centers on biblical truth, but it is spontaneous and revelatory.

CHAPTER 5 EXERCISE

ACTIVATION EXERCISE: ALLOW 10 MINUTES PER EXERCISE.

Purpose: *to assist students in becoming comfortable ministering to those in authority*

Select five students to minister to you (the Instructor). Ask the class to pray in the spirit and with an understanding. Have the student stand before you and release what they hear, see, or sense. Ask someone to write down or record each word.

Confidence Building

Purpose: *to gain insight and build their confidence about how their peers see them*

Have students sit in a circle. Select one student to stand behind a person in the circle. Ask everyone to close their eyes and focus. NO talking! The person standing is to ask God for an adjective that describes them. Once they receive it, they go from person to person, whispering it in everyone's ear. For example, words like "happy," "joyful," and "beautiful." Allow each student an opportunity to share their thoughts.

Five Methods of Prophesying
Chapter 5 Worksheet

Purpose: to comprehend and understand the various ways in which prophecy operates

1. What is the Spirit of Prophecy?

____

____

____

____

____

1. List the Nine Spiritual Gifts

_____________________ , _____________________

_____________________ , _____________________

_____________________ , _____________________ .

3. Are prophets the only ones who are anointed to prophecy while the Spirit of Prophecy is present? Yes or No? _____________________

Please explain.

____

____

____

____

____

4. Give an instance of someone who prophesied while the Spirit of Prophecy was present, along with scriptural references.

____

____

____

____

5. What does the Gift of Prophecy provide?

__________________________, __________________________

__________________________, __________________________.

6. List three ways in which the Gift of Prophecy operates.

__________________________, __________________________

__________________________, __________________________.

7. What is Prophetic Presbytery?

____

____

____

____

____

8. Name three ways in which the Prophetic Presbytery functions.

____

____

____

____

____

9. List three things that impacted you in this teaching.

a) ____

____

____

b) ____

____

____

c) ____

____

____

CHAPTER 06

OFFICE OF THE PROPHET

The purpose of this lesson is to discover the various characteristics, functions, and methods that Old and New Testament prophets operated in.

Though all prophets are called by God, not all are created equal. Their roles, functions, and assignments may vary from prophet to prophet.

Amos 3:7 (KJV): "Surely the Lord GOD will do nothing, but He revealeth His secret unto His servants the prophets."

Primary Functions of Prophets:

They speak on behalf of God; they are God's mouthpiece in the earth realm (Deuteronomy 18:18–19).

They are to edify, exhort, and comfort the body of Christ (1 Cor. 14:3).

OLD TESTAMENT PROPHET

Old and New Testament prophets share many similarities, yet their functions differ.

Function of Old Testament Prophets:

1. The Old Testament prophets were forth-tellers; they were to denounce sin, call for repentance, and warn Israel of pending judgment.

2. They were also foretellers. They predicted future events.

3. They functioned as watchmen (Ezekiel 33:6–7).

4. They gave a warning to the people of Israel (Ezekiel 3:17).

5. Old Testament prophets were used for guidance. They guided kings, people, and nations (1 Sam 22:5).

6. But the prophet Gad said to David, "Do not stay in the stronghold. Go into the land of Judah." So, David left and went to the forest of Hereth.

7. Old Testament Prophets were used to utter and write the infallible Scripture (2 Timothy 3:16, 17).

8. They reproved sin in individuals and the nation.

9. They pronounced the judgments of God.

10. They were entrusted with prophecy to the nations; Isaiah, Jeremiah, and Ezekiel each prophesied to the surrounding nations (Isaiah 13–21, Jer. 46–51, Ezek. 25–32).

11. Old Testament prophets were often used to appoint and anoint kings.

   - Nathan anointed Solomon as King (1 Kings 1:38–39).
   - Elijah anointed Jehu King over Israel (1 Kings 19:16; 2 Kings 9:1–10).
   - Elijah anointed Elisha to succeed him as prophet (1 Kings 19:16, 19).

12. Old Testament prophets prophesied regularly to kings.

13. Old Testament prophets were required to be 100 percent accurate, or the consequence was death (Deut. 18:20).

New Testament Prophet

FUNCTION OF NEW TESTAMENT PROPHETS:

1. New Testament prophets primarily operate as forth-tellers.

2. They can operate as foretellers to predict future events.

3. They are foundational gifts along with the Apostles (Ephesians 2:20).

4. Prophets confirm the already revealed will of God (Acts 13:1–3).

5. They are second in the divine order of the church, but not second in administration and authority. All gifts are equal in authority (1 Corinthians 12:28; Ephesians 4:11).

6. Prophets strengthen and or confirm local assemblies (Acts 15:32–41).

7. Their role is to help believers grow and serve in ministry (Ephesians 4:12).

8. No New Testament prophet was ever used to guide, control, or govern a believer concerning the will of God. However, it is often used to confirm the already known and revealed will of God.

9. No New Testament prophet was ever used in the utterance or writing of Scripture. All prophetic utterances were judged by the Word of Scripture (1 Corinthians 14:29–30, 32).

10. New Testament prophets do not usually give direction. That is the work of the Holy Spirit in the believer (Acts 21:10–11).

11. New Testament prophets are instructed to judge each other's prophetic words (1 Cor. 14:29; 1 Thes. 5:19–21).

New Testament Prophets Operate in the Following Functions:

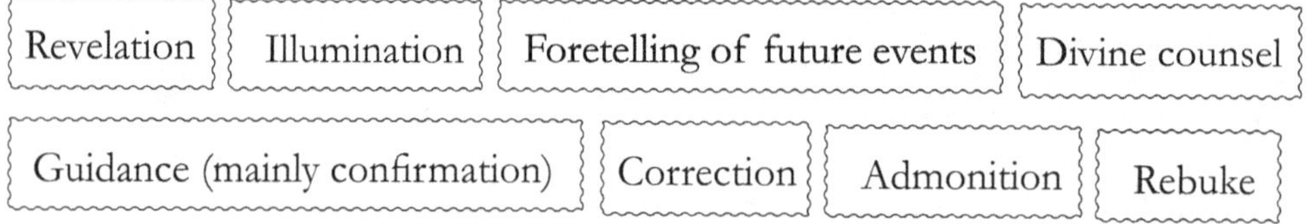

DIFFERENT TYPES OF PROPHETS

Not all prophets are created equal! They have various gifts, callings, and functions.

Hebrews 1:1 (NIV): "In the past God spoke to our ancestors through the prophets at many times and in various ways,"

Speaking or Oral Prophets

There were thirty-eight speaking/verbal prophets in the Old Testament.

Speaking or Verbal Prophets

1. Enoch (Jude 1:14)

2. Abraham (Genesis 20:7)

3. Moses (Deut. 18:18–22, 34:10–12)

4. Miriam and Aaron (Ex. 15:20; Num. 12:1–8)

5. Elijah (1 Kings 18:36; 1 Kings 19:16)

6. Joshua (Josh. 1, 23, 24)

7. Deborah (Jud. 4:4–5)

8. Elisha (1Kings 19:16, 19–20)

9. The four daughters of Philip (Acts 21:9)

10. Agabus (Acts 21:10)

11. Nathan, who confronted David (2 Samuel 7:2–3)

12. Micaiah, who saw the Lord sitting on His throne (1 Kings 22)

13. Ahijah, who condemned Jeroboam (1 Kings 14)

Writing Prophets:

1. Isaiah wrote of Uzziah's reign (2 Chron 26:22).

2. The prophet Iddo recorded the events of Abijah's reign (2 Chron 13:22).

3. Samuel the seer, Nathan the prophet, and Gad the seer recorded the events of King David's (1 Chron 29:29–30).

   A prophet was considered major or minor because of the length of the book written.

4. Major Writing Prophets: Jeremiah, Ezekiel, and Daniel

5. Minor Writing Prophets: Hosea, Joel, Amos, Obadiah, Jonah, Micah, Nahum, Habakkuk, Zephaniah, Haggai, Zechariah, and Malachi

PROPHETIC DEMONSTRATIONS /ACTS

A prophetic act is a divinely inspired physical act done as a demonstration in the natural (physical) realm to bring forth a prophetic release of the power of God that would be manifested in the natural realm.

A prophetic act or demonstration is simply demonstrating in the natural what you see or hear in the spiritual realm.

>> Isaiah walked naked for three years (Isaiah 20:2–3).

>> Isaiah soaked the altar with water (1 Kings 18:33–35).

>> Moses and Joshua removed their shoes while standing upon holy ground (Exodus 3:5; Joshua 5:15).

>> Solomon spread his hands toward heaven during the dedicatory prayer of the temple (1 Kings 8:22).

>> Elijah divided the waters of the Jordan River by smiting them with his mantle (2 Kings 2:8).

>> Elisha cast salt into a spring to heal its bitter water (2 Kings 2:19–21).

>> Abraham took a heifer, a she-goat, and a ram and "divided them in the midst and laid each piece one against another" (Genesis 15:10).

>> Joshua stretched a spear toward the city of Ai (Joshua 8:18–19).

>> Ahijah tore a new garment into twelve pieces (1 Kings 11:29–31).

>> Isaiah wrote the name Mahershalalhashbaz upon a scroll (which was to be the name of his unborn child). He united with his wife, the prophetess, and she bore a son (Isaiah 8:1–4).

>> Jeremiah placed stones in a brick kiln (Jeremiah 43:8–13).

>> Ezekiel ate a scroll (Ezekiel 2:8–3:6).

>> Hosea married a harlot to symbolize Israel's adultery (Hosea 1:1–2).

FALSE PROPHETS

Just as there are true prophets, there are false prophets.

Definition: In religion, a false prophet or pseudoprophet is a person who falsely claims the gift of prophecy or divine inspiration, or to speak to God, or who makes such claims for evil ends (Wikipedia).

Matthew 24:24 (NKJV): "For false Christs and false prophets will arise and show great signs and wonders; so much so that, if it were possible, they would deceive even the elect."

Matthew 7:15 (NKJV): "Beware of false prophets who come to you in sheep's clothing, but inwardly they are ravenous wolves."

The New Testament warns us to beware of False Prophets (Acts 13:6; 2 Peter 2:1; 1 John 4:1).

CHARACTERISTICS OF FALSE PROPHETS

A New Testament prophet isn't considered false simply because the prophetic word didn't come to pass. Many other attributes characterize a false prophet.

False prophets bear bad fruit, their motives and actions are evil, and they encourage evil and disobedience to the Lord. They sow distrust, discord, confusion, gossip, useless disputes, and incite division within the church (Romans 16:17–18).

> » **Matthew 7:15–17 (NKJV):** "Beware of false prophets, who come to you in sheep's clothing, but inwardly they are ravenous wolves. You will know them by their fruits. Do men gather grapes from thornbushes or figs from thistles? Even so, every good tree bears good fruit, but a bad tree bears bad fruit."

A prophet's words are false if they are inconsistent and contradict the Bible.

> » **Jeremiah 23:16 (NKJV):** "Thus says the Lord of hosts: Do not listen to the words of the prophets who prophesy to you. They make you worthless; they speak a vision of their own heart, not from the mouth of the Lord."

> » **Jeremiah 23:26 (NKJV):** "How long shall this be in the heart of the prophets who prophesy lies? they are prophets of the deceit of their own heart;"

> » **2 Peter 2:1 (NKJV):** "But there were also false prophets among the people, even as there will be false teachers among you, who secretly will bring in destructive heresies, even denying the Master who bought them, bringing on themselves swift destruction."

False prophets, teachings, and prophesying lead people away from the Lord.

> » **Deu 13:1–3 (NIV):** "If a prophet, or one who foretells by dreams, appears among you and announces to you a sign or wonder, and if the sign or wonder spoken of takes place, and the prophet says, 'Let us follow other gods' (gods you have not known) 'and let us worship them,' you must not listen to the words of that prophet or dreamer. The Lord your God is testing you to find out whether you love him with all your heart and with all your soul."

False prophets are characterized by a presumptuous, proud, and insolent attitude.

> » **Deu. 18:20 (NKJV):** "But a prophet who presumes to speak in my name anything I have not commanded, or a prophet who speaks in the name of other gods, is to be put to death."

False prophets are known for teaching false doctrine. Their teachings often fail to align with the foundational doctrines of Christianity, causing confusion and division within the church.

But there were also false prophets among the people, just as there will be false teachers among you. They will secretly introduce destructive heresies, even denying the sovereign Lord who bought them—bringing swift destruction on themselves. Many will follow their depraved conduct and will bring the way of truth into disrepute. In their greed, these teachers will exploit you with fabricated stories (2 Peter 2:1–3, NIV).

False prophets may have been recognized as genuine prophets of the Lord, but their disobedience eventually led them astray (1 Kings 13:11–32).

False prophets are consistently inaccurate in their prophesying. They prophesy lies rather than the word of God (Jeremiah 14:14; Ezekiel 13).

False prophets are motivated by the spirit of Mammon. They often seek personal gain and recognition, placing their own ambitions above the truth of God's word (1 Tim. 6:10; Jude 1:11).

False prophets can and will demonstrate signs and wonders to deceive.

- » **Matthew 24:23–25 (NIV):** "At that time if anyone says to you, 'Look, here is the Messiah!' or, 'There he is!' do not believe it. For false messiahs and false prophets will appear and perform great signs and wonders to deceive, if possible, even the elect. See, I have told you ahead of time."

- » False prophets claim unique spiritual insight or divine authority, but their messages ultimately lead to confusion and division among believers.

- » They are hyper-spiritual in conversations and believe that God tells them everything. "The Lord said to me…" or "God told me…" False prophets are motivated by a need to be noticed.

False prophets commonly use fear to motivate people.

- » **1 John 4:18 (NIV):** "There is no fear in love, but perfect love casts out fear. For fear has to do with punishment, and whoever fears has not been perfected in love."

- » False prophets are not in a covenant relationship with the Body of Christ (1 Peter 5:8).

- » They're not submitted to a local church or pastor.

- » They usually don't attend church at all, and if they do, their motives are often disingenuous.

- » They often operate without accountability and reject correction.

False prophets frequently operate without accountability, rejecting correction or guidance from mature believers. Their teachings often fail to align with the foundational doctrines of Christianity, causing confusion and division within the church. By distancing themselves from genuine fellowship and oversight, they create an environment where deception can thrive unchecked.

EXAMPLES OF FALSE PROPHETS IN THE OLD TESTAMENT:

» Hananiah prophesied that the exiles would return soon, contradicting God's message of judgment on Israel (Jeremiah 28:15–17).

» Balaam prophesied out of greed and led Israel into sin (Numbers 22–24, Revelation 2:14).

» Zedekiah prophesied peace and prosperity, conflicting with Jeremiah's prophecy from the Lord (Jeremiah 28:10–11).

EXAMPLES OF FALSE PROPHETS IN THE NEW TESTAMENT:

» Paul confronts and pronounces judgment on Bar-Jesus, who was a false prophet (Acts 13:6–11).

» False prophets are mentioned in Revelation. However, they are not named (Rev 16:13; Rev 19:20; Rev 20:10).

CHAPTER 6 EXERCISE

ACTIVATION EXERCISE: ALLOW 20 MINUTES FOR EACH EXERCISE.

Purpose: *to understand that God is all-knowing and he can give you a word for someone that you don't know personally*

Sit and meditate on the word of God. Ask the Holy Spirit to speak a word into your heart for someone. Grab a pen and paper and write the prophetic word without knowing who you will give it to. Ask God how He sees that person, what His heart is for that person, how He feels for that person? Write it down. Now, ask God who this word is for and give it to them.

Purpose: *to allow students to understand that God doesn't minister only to those whom you like or are in a good relationship with. God's heart is always to reconcile and restore relationships.*

Think of the person who is causing you the greatest amount of grief now. This may be a coworker, family member, or someone else. Ask God to bless them and reveal His heart for them through you. Ask God for a prophetic word or picture and then share it with them.

Office of the Prophet
Chapter 6 Worksheet

Purpose: to discover the various characteristics, functions, and methods that Old and New Testament prophets operated in

1. Name three functions of the Old Testament prophets. Give scriptural references.

a) ____

____

____

____

____

b) ____

____

____

____

____

c) ____

____

____

____

____

2. Name three functions of New Testament prophets. Give scriptural references.

a) ____

____

____

____

____

b) ____

c) ____

3. How many speaking or verbal prophets were there in the Old Testament?

____

4. Name five speaking prophets.

_______________________ , _______________________
_______________________ , _______________________
_______________________ .

5. Name three writing prophets.

_______________________ , _______________________
_______________________ .

6. What books did they write?

_______________________ , _______________________
_______________________ .

7. What is the difference between a major and a minor prophet?

____

____

____

8. Define prophetic demonstration/acts.

____

____

____

____

____

9. Name three prophets who used prophetic acts. What were they? Give scriptural reference.

a) _______________________________________

____

____

____

____

b) _______________________________________

____

____

____

____

c) _______________________________________

____

____

____

____

10. Define a false prophet?

____

____

____

____

____

11. Name three characteristics of a false prophet.

a) ____

____

____

____

____

b) ____

____

____

____

____

c) ____

____

____

____

____

Notes:

____

____

____

____

____

____

____

____

____

____

____

CHAPTER 07

PROPHETIC ETIQUETTE

1 Corinthians 14:40 (NKJV): "But let all things be done decently and in order."

1 Corinthians 14:32 (NKJV): "and the spirits of the prophets are subject to the prophets;"

Prophetic ministry is to bring edification, exhortation, and comfort to God's people (1 Corinthians 14:3)!

PROPHETIC MINISTRY PROTOCOL

Practical Application

1. Be yourself! Don't try to imitate another person's voice, mannerisms, or personality.

2. Speak clearly and loudly so everyone can hear you.

3. Don't use slang (unless prompted by the Holy Spirit). Remember, other cultures may not understand the meaning of your words.

4. If you have a word that is of an intimate nature for someone, share that in private, not over the microphone.

5. Don't slouch when standing before the audience. Stand erect and hold the microphone (if provided) with confidence.

6. Don't beat the microphone or say, "Testing, testing, testing."

7. Don't preface what you're about to release with a dissertation of your own. Release the word and sit down.

8. Don't sing the song of the Lord if you don't have a melodious voice for singing.

9. If you're a Prophetic Seer and need to describe a vision or dream, be mindful of how long you take, especially if you're in a public setting. Try to keep your time to two to three minutes.

10. If you're serving on a team, be cognizant of others ministering with you. Don't covet the microphone or try to give the entire word.

11. If you're in another spiritual house other than your own, do find out the prophetic protocol of that house before standing to release a prophetic word. The protocol varies from house to house.

12. Control your emotions when releasing a prophetic word. Remember, the Holy Spirit is subject to you, and He is a gentleman and will not overstep boundaries.

13. Don't preach your prophetic word. This is not the moment to showcase your preaching skills.

14. If possible, ensure that the prophetic word is recorded for accountability purposes. If it's a personal word, ask people to bring their phone and record.

15. Don't give parking lot or bathroom prophecies. Everything should be done decently and in order.

16. Remain open to correction and maintain a teachable spirit.

17. Don't wear jewelry (e.g., bracelets) that's loud and clangs, as this will distract people when you move your arms.

18. Avoid using repetitive words during prophetic ministry.

19. Use plain language. For example, avoid "Thus saith the Lord."

(20) Timing is everything! You may have a valid prophetic word; however, releasing it at the wrong time may cause disruption rather than acceptance.

(21) Be sensitive to the flow of the service. The Holy Spirit moves in conjunction with the natural flow.

PERSONAL HYGIENE

1. Do keep breath mints available. Be mindful of your breath at all times. While you may have an accurate word, if your breath is offensive, it could be a distraction to the person receiving it.

2. Make sure your attire is neat, clean, and presentable. Remember, you're the vessel through which God has chosen to speak. However, if your attire detracts from the word of God, they will only recall what you were wearing, not the words you spoke.

3. Be mindful of over using, perfume, or cologne. Some people are extremely sensitive to smells. So, don't allow your fragrance to overpower.

PROTOCOL FOR HOUSE PROPHETS

A house prophet is an individual designated by senior leadership to serve as the prophetic voice for a specific spiritual house. In no way does this imply that only one prophetic voice may serve as house prophet. A single house may have multiple house prophets and several prophetic teams.

(1) Be familiar with the protocol established by the leadership of the house.

(2) If no protocol has been established, consult with senior leadership to help establish guidelines.

(3) Always remain teachable and submitted to leadership.

Protocol for Prophetic People Releasing a Word in Another House

If the Lord gives you a word and you're not sure of the protocol for that house to release the word, then don't.

> » First, find someone in authority and inquire about the protocol.
>
> » Second, if you've never been to this house before, it may be necessary to write out the word and submit it to the house's leadership.
>
> » Third, if allowed to release the words corporately, remember that you're not there to bring correction or rebuke. Stay within the boundaries of edification, exhortation, and comfort.

Notes:

____

____

____

____

____

____

____

____

____

____

CHAPTER 7 EXERCISE

ACTIVATION EXERCISE: ALLOW 20–30 MINUTES FOR EXERCISE.

Purpose: *to establish students in the team ministry concept*

Prophetic Ministry to Volunteers: You will prophesy as a team of three to four.

Instructor: *First, find people outside your group and ask if they would be willing to volunteer for 10 minutes in return for receiving a blessing.*

Assign students to teams of three to four to minister prophetically to the volunteers for 10 minutes. Ask the volunteers to sit in front of the team and bring their phones for recording. (Student may sit as well.) Ask students to take turns releasing a prophetic word to the volunteers. Place specific emphasis on them flowing together as a team and building on each other's prophecy.

Pray with the volunteers before and after the session. Provide the volunteers with the opportunity to offer feedback and ask questions if necessary.

CHAPTER 08

PROPHETIC TEAMS AND PRESBYTERY

Amos 3:7 (NKJV): "Surely the Lord GOD does nothing, unless He reveals His secret to His servants the prophets."

WHAT ARE PROPHETIC TEAMS?

Prophetic Teams are a function of the local church designed to strengthen, edify, and encourage the body (1 Corinthians 14:3–4).

A prophetic team is a group of people who co-labor together in a local church body for the express purpose of advancing the Kingdom of God.

In the Old Testament, prophetic ministry frequently functioned as a collaborative endeavor, with prophets and prophets in training working together in teams.

There were "schools of prophets" at Jericho, Gilgal, Ramah, Bethel, and Gibeah (2 Kings 2:3; 2 Kings 4:38; 2 Kings 2:5).	Saul encountered a "band of prophets" at the school of prophets in Gibeah (1 Samuel 10:9–12).

- » Jesus was the perfect model for team ministry. He rarely ministered without the disciples nearby (John 20:21–22).

- » Jesus formed teams and sent them out in groups of two, twelve, seventy, and seventy-two (Mark 6:7; Luke 10:1–24).

- » Paul took several missionary journeys with his team.

- » Peter and John were viewed as a team within the larger team, commonly acting together (Acts 3:1, 11, 4:13).

EXAMPLES OF PROPHETIC TEAMS:

- » **Agabus and others** (Acts 11:27–30)

- » **Barnabus, Simeon, Lucius, Manaen, Saul** (Acts 13:1)

- » **Judas and Silas** (Acts 15:32)

- » **Philip's four daughters** (Acts 21:8–11)

- » **Timothy and Erastus** (Acts 19:22)

"Coming together is a beginning. Staying together is progress. Working together is success."

Team Ministry was the method the early church used to evangelize and disciple Nations.

BENEFITS OF PROPHETIC TEAM MINISTRY:

- » Team Ministry enables the prophetic word to be evaluated for accuracy and balance by other prophets (1 Corinthians 14:32). Let two or three prophets speak, and let the others assess what is said.

- » No one has the full counsel of God; therefore, we need other prophets to release their part (1 Corinthians 13:9). For we know in part, and we prophesy in part.

» Unity and purpose are the keys to a successful prophetic team.

DEVELOPING A COHESIVE PROPHETIC TEAM

1. Selecting Prophetic Team Members

The first step in developing a cohesive team is careful selection of team members. This should be done with senior leadership's approval.

Criteria for Selecting Prophetic Team Members:

» Must be a born-again believer

» Must be Spirit-filled

» Must have a proven track record of faithful attendance in church

» Must serve or have served in other areas of ministry in the local church

» Must be an intercessor

» Be faithful in duties and responsibilities

» Must walk in godly character and integrity

» Must be accountable to leadership

» Must be teachable and open to correction

» Must be knowledgeable of the Word of God

» Must release accurate prophetic words

» Must not be a novice

» Must have completed School of the Prophets Training

» Must continue with prophetic development

Wisdom Nugget:
Unity is strength...
when there is teamwork
and collaboration,
wonderful things
can be achieved.

2. Know the Vision

It is essential for teams to function cohesively. All members must clearly understand both the corporate vision and the prophetic ministry vision outlined by senior leadership (Hab. 2:2).

3. Communication, Communication, Communication

Effective communication is essential for developing a successful team. Prophetic ministry, unlike any other ministry, is highly susceptible to the attack of the enemy to bring in confusion, strife, envy, jealousy, and most of all division (James 3:16).

4. Trust

Developing trust among team members is essential if the team is to flourish. Trust is the bedrock of every successful relationship.

5. Conflict Resolution

Conflicts will arise amongst team members. However, address them promptly and efficiently. Don't allow offenses to fester as they tend to grow (Luke 17:1).

6. Encourage Feedback

Team leaders, be mindful to encourage team members to provide feedback on how the team is functioning. This helps foster engagement in the prophetic team process. Remember: this is team ministry—everyone has a voice.

7. Know Those Who Labor Among You!

As team members, it is essential that you truly know one another—not just through ministerial roles, but also relationally (1 Thess. 5:12).

8. Beware of the Jezebel Spirit

The prophetic ministry is highly susceptible to this spirit. This spirit hates the prophetic and seeks to kill prophets. Don't presume that a Jezebel spirit only manifests itself in women. It is a spirit that operates in both men and women (1 Kings 18:13; Rev 2:20).

> "Remember teamwork begins by building trust. And the only way to do that is to overcome our need for invulnerability."
> Patrick Lencioni

PROPHETIC PRESBYTERY

Neglect not the gift that is in thee, which was given thee by prophecy, with the laying on of the hands of the presbyter (1 Tim. 4:14).

The word presbytery refers to a group of ministers and elders.

Strong's Greek #4244—presbytérion: properly, a council or group of elders—a team of overseers serving a local church who lead, feed, and shepherd the people of the Lord.

126

A prophetic presbytery team consists of elders and/or prophets with a mature prophetic gift, assembled to minister prophetically to one or more people. (The team is normally appointed by senior leadership.) This type of ministry typically involves the laying on of hands.

Presbytery teams are assembled to minister prophetically for various reasons:

- » To seek prophetic revelation, clarification, and confirmation for those called to leadership in the church (Acts 13:1–3)

- » To ordain someone into the fivefold ministry (Titus 1:5)

- » To confirm and activate someone's gifting, calling, and place of ministry in the Body (Acts 6:3;, Acts 6:6)

- » To confirm and activate them in Christian ministry (Acts 14:21–22)

- » To ordain elders to ministry (Acts 14:23)

- » To minister a prophetic rhema word of God to individuals

Ministers and other church leaders (as designated) can prophesy over an individual while serving on the presbytery team.

Notes:

____

____

____

____

____

____

____

____

____

____

____

CHAPTER 8 EXERCISE

ACTIVATION EXERCISE: ALLOW 20–30 MINUTES FOR THE EXERCISE.

Team Ministry Purpose: *to develop a strong, cohesive team*

Exercise One:

Purpose: *This exercise is designed to help teams get to know their teammates beyond the ministry.*

Divide groups into teams of four. Have each person share five personal things about themselves. Share for no longer than three minutes per person, i.e., marital status, how many children you have, hobbies, etc. Now, one at a time, repeat at least three things you learned about your teammate.

Exercise Two:

Purpose: *to develop team members to sense, see, and hear individually but connect the pieces to see the whole counsel of God concerning a particular area*

Group students into teams of four to six. Give each group a specific topic to pray for, such as pastors, couples, lost souls, a township, a city, or a nation, etc. Make sure there is a scribe for each group. Have the team pray in the Spirit for approximately two to three minutes, focusing on their assignment. Quiet them for approximately two to three minutes. Now ask each team member to share what they sensed, saw, or heard. Make sure to write down each.

As they share, ask them to connect the individual words, visions, etc., to form a complete picture of the counsel of God concerning this assignment. It's okay if they didn't receive a complete picture.

Allow students to continue praying over this assignment for one week and to journal their reflections on what they receive. At the next class, ask them to meet with their group and share their revelation.

End Notes:

References:

Chapter 1

Damazio, Frank. *Seasons of Intercession*. Portland, OR: City Bible Publishing, 1998.

Harper, Douglas. *Online Etymology Dictionary*. 2010.

Femrite, Tommi, Elizabeth Alves, and Karen Kaufman. *Intercessors*. Ventura, CA: Regal Books, a Division of Gospel Light, 2000.

Chapter 2

Early, Tim, and Theresa Early. *The School of the Prophets*. Global Leadership Institute, n.d., 16.

"Discernment." *Merriam-Webster.com*. Merriam-Webster. Accessed June 14, 2016.

Collins English Dictionary – Complete and Unabridged. 12th ed. Glasgow: HarperCollins, 2014. Originally published 1991, 1994, 1998, 2000, 2003, 2006, 2007, 2009, 2011. Accessed June 14, 2016. http://www.thefreedictionary.com/discern.

Chapter 3

Blanchard, Tim. *A Practical Guide to Finding Your Spiritual Gifts*. Wheaton, IL: Tyndale House, 1983.

Hagin, Kenneth. *The Holy Spirit and His Gifts*. Tulsa, OK: RHEMA Bible Church (Kenneth Hagin Ministries), 1991.

HELPS Word-Studies. Interpretation. Helps Ministries, Inc., 1987, 2011.

Chapter 4

Eckhardt, John. "The Shamar Prophet." *Impact Network*. Accessed November 30, 2025. www.impactnetwork.

Goll, Jim. *The Coming Prophetic Revolution*. Grand Rapids, MI: Chosen Books, 2001.

Hagin, Kenneth. *The Ministry Gifts*. Broken Arrow, OK: Rhema Bible Training Center, 1991.

NAS Exhaustive Concordance of the Bible with Hebrew-Aramaic and Greek Dictionaries. La Habra, CA: The Lockman Foundation, 1981, 1998.

Russell, John E. *Ephesians*, 2003–2004. www.jcrministries.org.

Smith, William. *Smith's Bible Dictionary*. 1901. www.biblestudytools.com.

Vine, W. E. *Vine's Expository Dictionary of New Testament Words*. Various definitions retrieved online, 1134–1135.

Chapter 6

Early, Tim, and Theresa Early. *The School of the Prophets*. Global Leadership Institute, 1998.

Pounds, Wil. "Message." *Saved by Grace in Christ*. 2008. www.sbideinchrist.org.

Suggested Reading:

Becoming a Prayer Warrior by Elizabeth Alves

Discerner by James Goll

Exploring Your Dreams and Visions by James Goll

The Seer by James Goll

The Voice of God by Cindy Jacobs

Prophetic Intercession by Barbara Wentroble

About Wanda Roberson

Wanda Roberson is a devoted wife, loving mother, and proud grandmother whose life is deeply rooted in her family. Her unwavering commitment to her loved ones is paralleled by her passion and dedication to ministry.

Wanda faithfully serves at The EmPowerment Center Church in Katy, Texas, where she co-pastors alongside her husband, Apostle David O. Roberson. She was ordained to the Office of Prophet in 1995. Her message is one of hope, encouragement, inspiration, and deliverance. As an Apostolic Prophet, she has  traveled the nations (South Africa, Zimbabwe, Nigeria, Canada, South Korea, and the United Kingdom) assisting in establishing churches in present truth, laying an apostolic foundation, and bringing the fullness of God's love, hope, wisdom and balance to His people.

Wanda is also the Founder and President of Wanda Roberson Ministries (WRM). This multi-faceted international prophetic ministry is designed to teach, train, and develop prophetic people for the end-time harvest, equipping people around the world to fulfill their spiritual calling and purpose.

She established a School of the Prophets in South Africa and hosts Prophetic Conferences as well as Prophetic Training Summits throughout the Nations.